My Life In

INSTITUTIONS

AND MY WAY OUT

MICHAEL JOSEPH KENNEDY

In collaboration with Sue Lehr, Janet M. Duncan & Sherry Foehr

Produced by:

FriesenPress
Suite 300 – 852 Fort Street
Victoria, BC, Canada V8W 1H8

www.friesenpress.com

Distributed to the trade by The Ingram Book Company

Table of Contents

Albert Einstein reminded us all:

"The world is a dangerous place to live, not because of the people who are evil, but because of those people who don't do anything about it."

I want to dedicate this book to my wife, Lori Kennedy, my mom, my brothers and my sister for always being there for me. I also want to dedicate this book to the memory of Hank Bersani Jr. He was a great friend and he helped me a lot to become the person I am today.

Acknowledgments

This book would not have been possible without the contributions of all the people that believed in me even when the system did not. The so-called "system" did not believe that I was capable of making something of myself but the following people did. I would like to give many thanks to my wife, Lori A. Kennedy, who has encouraged me to tell my life story so that I could better the lives of other people. I would also like to thank my parents, both of my brothers, and my sister for all of the love and support that they have given me throughout the years. A few of my friends and co-workers, including Joyce Becker, Corkie Langley, Harold Johnson, David Schipe, Doris Moore, Jerry Passamonte, Jennifer Collins, and their families played an important role in who I am today as a person. I would also like to thank the director of Center on Human Policy at Syracuse University, Steven J. Taylor, along with all of the staff past and present, especially Cyndy Colavita and Rachel Zubal. I want to acknowledge and thank self-advocates Karen Gillette and Sally Johnston. Most of these people were able to speak with Sue Lehr and Janet Duncan over a four-year period to create this book. Sue and Janet did all the research and put together the book with my words. Finally, I want to dedicate this book in memory of Hank Bersani Jr. Hank taught me a lot when I first started my job in self-advocacy.

Preface

I am writing this book to tell a true story from a person who was born in the early 1960s, who has cerebral palsy and who does not want to be seen for his disability, but rather as a person. I am writing this book to show people who work within the human services system that people with disabilities are people, and that their disabilities are secondary. I also want this book to be used for training purposes, so that people with disabilities can learn how to advocate for themselves, and for the people that provide direct care to use this as a learning tool, to help treat people with disabilities as people. My hopes are that despite our unique needs, people can, for once, look beyond what is on the outside and discover that we have gifts just like everyone else.

I want to make it clear that this book is not meant to draw attention to myself or to make people pity me, but to show society that people with all types of disabilities have a purpose, and that we can make a difference in this world, if given the chance.

This book was several years in the making, with interviews being conducted during good times as well as during illness and struggle. It represents a continuation of my story, with many false starts, and finally an ending. But really my story is just the beginning for many people with disabilities. I hope today's young children with disabilities never go through what my family went through. We have to keep watch and learn from our mistakes.

Introduction

Wearing jeans, a red flannel shirt, work boots, and a winter jacket, Michael Kennedy looks the picture of health and vigor as he wheels around in his motorized wheelchair. Attached to his ear, a blinking blue light indicates his Bluetooth headset is ready for calls. His cropped, salt-and- pepper hair is smoothed under his wool National Guard cap. He greets us with enthusiasm, and parks himself facing the fireplace in the reception area of his condominium complex. He is the picture of a successful professional, who, according to his mother, "has it all together and is the most sensible one of the bunch."

Today, life is good for Michael Kennedy. It wasn't always this way; for the past thirty years Michael has fought for the right to participate in every decision made regarding where to live, with whom to spend his time, and how to contribute to his community. Michael has also worked all his adult life. Even before he completed his high school education he took a position at Syracuse University, at the Center on Human Policy, and he has continued to work in the field of self-advocacy ever since. Michael currently works for an agency in which he is responsible for self-advocacy training and policy development in New York State. Well-known as a social activist in Central New York, Michael is on a first-name basis with numerous local politicians. Through his professional activities, regular attendance at a variety of regional and national conferences and constant engagement with other self-advocates, he has built a reputation far beyond his own community for leading the efforts to empower people with disabilities.

Michael is now over fifty years old and he and his wife Lori have been married for more than twenty years. They recently moved into a fully accessible single family home in a suburb of Syracuse, New York. Together, Michael and Lori have dreams of retiring somewhere in the warm southern states, camping and visiting friends and family.[1] They look back on a good life together, but also on the darker time before they met, when Michael was confined in a series of residential institutions, denied education, adequate care and desperately needed therapies. They reflect on the circumstances that defined his life and the strategies he developed to make the best of them, to realize his dreams of living a life like the one he enjoys today.

This is Michael's story of his life as he remembers it, nuanced by the memories of his mother, Patricia Kennedy, his wife, Lori Kennedy, his brothers and sister and many other people who made a difference in his life. Over the course of Michael's adult life, he has told many parts of these stories to a variety of different audiences, always with the sincere intent of enabling them to see that decisions made for or about him were always colored by the fact that he has a disability. While this was not always a bad thing, in many instances the results were bad.

Times have changed somewhat since the early 1960s, when Michael was first sent to a nursing home at the age of three because there were no services or supports for his parents to keep him at home. Later, when he was placed in different state-run residential institutions, it was supposed to be what was best for him and his family. Today, we know that the conditions in these facilities were unhealthy, overcrowded and inhumane. Education was either non-existent or mediocre for young Michael and his future looked dismal as he matured. Like so many others he was destined to live and die "behind the walls" with no voice—but Michael began to realize that he could use his voice to tell the world about what was happening to him and other people with disabilities. He recognized the power of his voice to draw attention to the horrific conditions they endured. He realized he could plant the seeds for change.

Following Michael's story, this book traces the movement of disability rights, self-advocacy, and empowerment for those with disabilities. As Michael was fighting to make his voice heard, the public was beginning to learn about conditions inside institutions through exposés and news reports. This narrative represents our attempt to weave together text and context in the story of Michael's life. It is a story of triumph, yet there is a cautionary note in Michael's tale since we still live in precarious times for people with disabilities. Since the most horrific institutions were closed and it is now much more common for people with disabilities to live in the community, the public is less aware of the history of institutionalization and the kinds of abuses people with disabilities routinely suffered just a few decades ago. Pressure to optimize government spending makes it all too easy to forget the consequences of focusing solely on the bottom line when people's lives and livelihoods are at stake. Abuse can still happen anywhere, anytime, and we need to remain vigilant. Indeed, recent media exposés of neglect, abuse and even deaths of people with disabilities while in the care of the state should serve as a chilling reminder of how far we still need to go in our society. People with disabilities remain a fragile sector of our population and advocacy is more important than ever. The lessons we learn from the history of the disability rights movement, and from personal accounts of individuals like Michael, should alert us to the potential dangers inherent in all large residential institutions, including nursing homes. We cannot let history repeat itself.

1

His Mother Speaks and Michael Remembers

Michael Joseph Kennedy was born on October 27, 1960 in Ludlow, Massachusetts. He was the third child in his family.[2] Mrs. Kennedy was young, but frail, and none of her pregnancies were easy. Lynn, her eldest, was born prematurely and struggled as a baby and young child. Kevin, the next sibling, was bigger and sturdier, but when he was just three months old, Mrs. Kennedy became pregnant with Michael. Carrying Michael was particularly difficult, as she had not fully recovered from Kevin's birth. Mrs. Kennedy was sick throughout her pregnancy and exhausted from caring for the rest of her family while working nights in a local factory. "I wondered if I could carry him," Mrs. Kennedy related, remembering her fears in the months before Michael's birth.

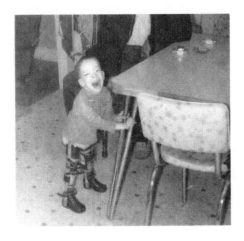

Standing at my Aunt & Uncle's table at their farm.

Viewing birds from the kitchen table.

The day she went into labor, her husband had already left for work as a truck driver for a local typewriter company. On the road, Mr. Kennedy was stopped by a state trooper who told him his wife was in the hospital. She was only in her sixth month of pregnancy and Mr. Kennedy was terrified. Mrs. Kennedy remembers, "He burned out his truck engine getting [to the hospital]." Mrs. Kennedy remembers little about her labor, but she does recall that Michael only weighed three pounds four ounces. The attending doctors noted that he was "markedly cyanotic" at birth, meaning that his skin had taken on a blue tinge resulting from insufficient oxygen. He was immediately admitted to the hospital's isolation unit. Mrs. Kennedy was discharged from the hospital three days after giving birth, but Michael remained in the hospital for the next fifty-two days. Once at home, he seemed to thrive. He took his bottle readily and seemed alert and aware of his surroundings.

The first hint that Michael was different from other babies came when it was time to introduce solid food. The problem was not that he was a fussy baby; he liked being given his bottle, but was also content to lie on his back on the floor with his bottle propped up next to him. Feeding him with a spoon proved a real problem, though. "He couldn't eat solid food. He would gag," Mrs. Kennedy recalled. Michael never picked up finger foods, either. Mrs. Kennedy knew that most one-year-olds could feed themselves, but she was reluctant to push Michael to eat regular food when it clearly made him choke. Mrs. Kennedy's mother criticized this decision. In her view, allowing Michael to lie around and drink from a bottle was just letting him be lazy. When Michael's mother refused to force Michael to eat solid foods, his grandmother accused her of trying to starve her baby. Mrs. Kennedy shrugged her shoulders as she recounted these discussions with her mother. "What could I do? I knew something was wrong, but what could I do? He never cried. I mean, he was really a good baby. [...] I would prop up a bottle and he was happy." And he seemed to be healthy – he looked around and made sounds like other babies.

Mrs. Kennedy did ask their family doctor about Michael's eating problems and described how he was content just lying on his back, watching the world go by. "I think he was an Army doctor," Mrs. Kennedy said, but she recalled little else. The doctor thought Michael might have cerebral palsy. When she asked what this was and what it meant for her son's future, the doctor replied, "He's spastic." He explained that some children like Michael would eventually be able to walk and talk, but he was not sure what Michael would be able to do.

When the doctor identified Michael as "spastic," he was probably referring to a medical diagnosis of "Spastic Diplegia," also called 'Little's Disease' after Dr. William John Little, who first described this children's neurological disorder in a paper published in 1861. Dr. Little, an English orthopedic surgeon, studied children whose arms and legs appeared to be deformed by rigid muscles and shortened tendons. These children had difficulty picking up or holding objects and many could neither walk nor crawl. Dr. Little described their uncontrolled movements as "spastic" and hypothesized that the condition resulted when a baby's brain was deprived of adequate oxygen during a difficult birth.[3]

Another British medical doctor coined the term "cerebral palsy" in the 1880s. This terminology, along with Dr. Little's publications, attracted the attention of the famed psychiatrist, Dr. Sigmund Freud, some of whose earliest works explored cerebral palsy. In 1897, Freud published his own research findings, which contradicted Little's causative theory. Freud hypothesized that cerebral palsy was the result of some sort of disruption during fetal development that occurred prior to the moment of birth. He explained that many spastic children also exhibited a variety of other problems, including mental retardation, seizures and visual problems that could not be explained by birth trauma.

Up through the 1920s, cerebral palsy was generally regarded as a neurological disorder and often confused with poliomyelitis. Following in the footsteps of Little and Freud, researchers tended to focus on identifying the cause rather than on improving the lives of people who had cerebral palsy. Most treatments involved surgery on nerves or muscles with the goal of reducing spasticity. Only in the 1930s did doctors begin to regard cerebral palsy as an orthopedic problem and focus on developing therapeutic approaches. The introduction of the Apgar score in 1953 encouraged physicians to evaluate infants right after birth and by the time Michael was born, experts agreed "that the clinical symptoms of cerebral palsy might be improved significantly through neurophysiological physiotherapy, especially if the therapy was started early."[4] Unfortunately for Michael, the assessment tool for infant reflexes that came to be the standard means to predict cerebral palsy was only developed in 1964, long after it could do him any good.[5]

When Michael was fifteen months old, his pediatrician suggested a professional evaluation. The Kennedys, who had moved from Massachusetts to New York State, took Michael to Ithaca Reconstruction Home[6] where clinical specialists spent two weeks observing Michael and performing tests. They concluded that Michael indeed had cerebral palsy and arranged for him to receive outpatient services to help him develop useful skills. He learned how to use a urinal and, with the aid of a wheelchair, gained some mobility. He also learned to talk – a skill he practiced avidly with anyone who would listen. He developed a strong personality and a good sense of humor that helped him deal with the frustration of not being able to control his arms and legs well.

Caring for Michael became more challenging as he grew. Although he could now eat solid food, it took him longer than the rest of the family and he often made a mess. Because his legs were so bent and constricted, he could not stand unassisted or walk at all. He could only scoot along the floor on his bottom using his hands for balance. He could not grasp much with his hands and potty training was still an unfulfilled dream. His tight muscles also caused him pain if he was not positioned correctly. The Kennedys' living situation compounded these problems. They lived in a third-floor walk-up apartment, so it was difficult to get Michael in and out of the house, especially for his petite mother. Mr. Kennedy worked a morning shift, driving a truck for a local typewriter manufacturer, while Mrs. Kennedy took care of the children. One income was not enough, though, so Mrs. Kennedy also worked the late shift at the typewriter factory, from three o'clock in the afternoon until midnight. Needless to say, neither parent got enough sleep, and the fact that caring for Michael was physically strenuous only made it more difficult. Michael noticed how evenings "started to be a lot of wear and tear" on his father, not only because it was hard work at the end of a long day, but also because he felt inadequate: "He wasn't quite sure how to do things so that he would not injure himself or me," Michael recalls.

When Michael was about four years old, the same doctor who had referred them to Ithaca Reconstruction Home suggested surgery for Michael's legs. He explained that during the surgery, the tendons that forcefully held Michael's legs in their constricted, crossed position would be cut and then his legs would be put into casts to allow the muscles to slowly strengthen and lengthen. There would be a bar between the leg casts, keeping them separate, to allow the hip joints and muscles to adjust. The doctor assured Michael's parents that the casts would only remain on for a few months, after which Michael would be fitted with leg braces and special shoes. The braces would be hinged at the knees, and, with these and physical therapy, Michael should be able to learn how to walk. A few months with Michael in casts would be difficult, but they hoped it would only be a brief episode in their lives. Soon Michael would be walking - a dream come true.

The surgery went well, but caring for Michael after the surgery was very hard on everyone in the family, especially because the youngest Kennedy child, Robbie, was on the way. Michael had to be carried everywhere and toileting was difficult with the cumbersome leg casts. Even after the casts were removed, the braces were not much better. His older sister, Lynn, remembers Michael crying and screaming, especially at night, when he had to try to sleep with the braces on. His legs and hip joints were sore and the stretching imposed by the braces was very painful. It was clear that he needed intensive physical therapy to strengthen his leg muscles and to help him learn to walk. During an extended stay at the Ithaca Reconstruction Home, Michael learned to use a walker to stabilize and support his upright position and he did eventually learn to walk with his leg braces on. Unfortunately, Michael's lower body, and especially his legs, never really grew strong enough to support his upper body weight. Without the walker, he could not stand on his own. Still, he was much more mobile than he had been before. He left the hospital with new braces and a new sense of independence.

The Kennedys' joy at Michael's success was short-lived, however. Although he had been fitted with orthopedic shoes when he got his new braces, he quickly outgrew both. Mrs. Kennedy is not sure why, but Michael was never given new shoes or braces after he outgrew his first pair: "Maybe our insurance ran out. I don't know. He just never got new braces or shoes after that." Without properly fitting braces or shoes, walking was simply out of the question. They tried their best to help Michael do the exercises the therapists suggested, but it was impossible to maintain a strict regimen. After more than a year of stress and pain, the Kennedys were back to where they had started: carrying Michael everywhere he needed to go. Even worse, school was out of the question. Michael was eager to learn but in the mid-1960s, there was no requirement that children with disabilities go to school, nor were schools obligated to make accommodations for disabled children who wished to attend school. The Kennedys arranged for a tutor to come in for an hour a day so Michael could learn the basics, but that was no substitute for formal education. Michael loved clowning around with his siblings and it was clear that he would love the social interaction that school could provide. Michael's parents were frustrated and the strain of caring for him and their other children while working full time was taking its toll on both of them. Mr. Kennedy's drinking increased, and Mrs. Kennedy's nerves were fraying. They did their best, but it was not enough, and all their attempts to improve the situation seemed to make no difference.

The family doctor pressed the Kennedys to consider placing Michael in the New York State Rehabilitation Hospital in West Haverstraw.[7] This hospital was dedicated to treating individuals with physical disabilities, especially those resulting from polio and cerebral palsy. The doctor explained that knowledgeable doctors at West Haverstraw would evaluate Michael to determine appropriate therapy protocols and design a treatment plan that would suit his physical needs. The Kennedys hated the idea of sending Michael to live in what was essentially a nursing home, but they trusted the doctor. They had no one else to offer advice and they knew that their son needed help they could not give him at home. They had been paying for everything Michael needed themselves and the costs were only getting higher. They worried that Michael had no opportunity to make friends at home. Even worse, they feared that they were denying him the chance to make the most of himself. The initial evaluation at the hospital suggested that after about two years of intensive physical therapy, Michael would improve enough that he could be discharged. This gave the Kennedys hope. Maybe, with the right therapy, their son would be able to walk on his own, be potty trained, and take care of himself – even attend school with his sister and brothers. Neither the doctors nor the staff told Michael's parents much about what Michael's life in West Haverstraw would be like, but they were convinced that it was his best option. Michael knows how hard this decision was for his parents. "My parents were told that they were holding me back, and I would not be able to grow," he explains. "So, even though they hated to make this decision, they made it. I think it destroyed them a little bit to do this."

Mr. and Mrs. Kennedy's high expectations when Michael was admitted to West Haverstraw were soon disappointed. Michael had not been there long before they were told that their little son was misbehaving. No one considered him a "good" boy anymore. According to the staff, Michael was very upset most of the time. He continually acted up, hitting other children, and even pushed one little boy's high chair over. In retrospect, this rebellious behavior appears to have been Michael's first act of self-advocacy.

The reality of life in West Haverstraw explains Michael's strong desire to leave. Reflecting on his first day there, Michael says, "I walked into Helen Hayes' Building as it is called now and I can still tell you, thirty-five years later, what the smell was like in that room. It was dark. It was dingy. The kids couldn't speak, they just sat around the day room. They basically had no dignity. After my first fifteen minutes there, I clenched on my father's leg so hard, I swear to God, today he's still got a scar on his leg from where I clenched. And if you want to talk about gut wrenching – he couldn't do anything because, once those papers were signed, my parents did not have any control what so ever!"

The longer Michael stayed at West Haverstraw, the more miserable he became. He was the only verbal child on his unit so he had no one to talk to except for the two staff members. Since they had to care for twenty children with disabilities on their own, they had nearly no time to chat and even less interest. It was not unusual for some of the children to miss meals because the staff simply did not get to them on time. Although Michael's parents believed the hospital would give him regular physical therapy, in fact most of his days were spent doing very little. Michael remembers the mind-numbing monotony of life at West Haverstraw: "you got up, you ate in groups, you went to activities in groups (what little activities they had), you ate at a certain time, you took showers together, there was no privacy." Even worse, the staff intimidated their charges and took out their frustration with the situation on the helpless children they were supposed to be caring for. "I grew up from a [...] boy into a man in a hurry and I mean just that. I didn't have any childhood. I had to learn right from the beginning if I was going to survive in this system. I had to become a fighter."

Michael spent most of his time at West Haverstraw looking forward to his next visit with his family. In addition to bringing Michael home for holidays like Christmas or Easter, Mr. Kennedy, a trucker, always tried to organize his routes so he could stop and see Michael when he was in the area. Sometimes he brought Mrs. Kennedy for a weekend. It was a long drive, but they believed it was worth it to make the trip and pay for a hotel room so they could take their son out and spend time with him. Michael's mother always waited at the hotel, though, because she "couldn't deal with the fact of going and seeing [her son] in a nursing home." Michael told his parents how much he hated West Haverstraw, but although they sympathized with him, the staff members they spoke with always had an explanation or excuse. The Kennedys essentially had no choice other than to trust the staff, who blamed every problem on Michael. In an era when parents were supposed to defer to medical professionals, it never occurred to them to question the assertions or decisions of the staff.

With no one to talk to and no incentive to behave the way staff wanted, Michael began to speak out more and more. He says, "two things [I learned there] stick out in my head, every single day of my life. Don't go looking for trouble, but don't let anyone ever walk all over you because if you do, you're done. When you know you're right, stick up for what you believe in." What Michael regarded as sticking up for what he believed in was generally interpreted as acting out by the staff. They could not keep him under control and they feared that his behavior would escalate to the point that "someone was going to get hurt." Soon after Michael turned nine years old, West Haverstraw administrators contacted his parents to request that they come and get him; the New York State Rehabilitation Hospital could no longer waste time and energy on a recalcitrant youngster when so many other children were ready and waiting for its intensive services.

When Michael's parents made their final trip to West Haverstraw to take him back home, they hoped to receive some information about how to continue the therapy Michael was supposedly undergoing —but they were disappointed again. Michael had made little progress in the years he spent there and the hospital staff offered neither useful information nor suggestions about other available resources to help Michael when he left. The only thing Mrs. Kennedy recalls being told was how to do some exercises to strengthen Michael's legs. She was also told that her young son was "mildly mentally retarded". The Kennedys had no idea what to do or where to turn. They took Michael home.

"Then nothing." Mrs. Kennedy said with a sigh as she told about this epoch in her life. "We kept Michael at home and things stayed pretty much the same."

After Michael returned, Mrs. Kennedy tried her best to do the exercises with Michael, but with three other children, a home to keep and a job, the Kennedys knew it was not enough. Mrs. Kennedy had developed medical problems while Michael was away and her health continued to decline. She and her husband searched for other sources of help and eventually decided to try the Shriners Hospital near Boston. The Shriners were supposed to aid "crippled children" like Michael.

Actually, the Shriners Hospitals for Children are only one part of the larger Shriners organization, an international community of Freemasons officially called the "Ancient Arabic Order of the Nobles of the Mystic Shrine" (AAONMS). Shriners Hospitals treat children with a variety of physical disabilities (such as cleft palates, burns and orthopedic and spinal cord injuries) although they were originally established for children with polio. Their services are free to children who are younger than eighteen and whose condition is considered treatable, regardless of their religion or race. For the Kennedys, the Shriners Hospital seemed to offer a real possibility to get Michael what he needed. They scheduled an appointment and traveled with Michael to a Shriners Hospital near Boston, a good five-hour drive from their home.

Once there, they waited with growing impatience as their appointed time came and went. "We sat there for five hours, *five* hours," Mrs. Kennedy emphasized, with an angry frown crossing her face as she told the story, "before someone finally saw Michael, and then it was only for five minutes. They didn't check him over. They didn't say anything, nothing. There was no conversation. We left." She paused, looked away, her eyes narrowed and her jaw hardened. When she spoke again, her voice was bitter. "I never gave any money to that crippled children's fund again."

And so the Kennedys took Michael home again, without any hope of getting the support they needed to keep him there or the services he needed to thrive. As they had done before, they scraped together money to pay for some in-home care and managed as best they could. Michael remembers spending lots of time watching cartoons on television while his siblings were at school and only occasionally having a therapist or tutor come to the house to work with him. Michael's siblings pitched in to help whenever they could. Even Robbie did his best. One time, as he was proudly pushing his brother's wheelchair down the street at top speed, Robbie failed to notice an uneven spot in the sidewalk. When the wheelchair hit the crack, it stopped short, sending Michael sailing through the air. Fortunately, he landed softly, and the story went down in the Kennedy family annals as "the time Robbie made Michael fly".

Even though everyone was trying to make it work, Mrs. Kennedy was increasingly worried about her own health and her husband's. It was also clear to her that her other children were suffering under the strain that caring for Michael brought. She knew they loved their brother, but she also recognized that they were beginning to resent Michael. It was especially hard for Lynn. She was the eldest and a girl, so a lot of the care giving fell on her shoulders, especially when Mrs. Kennedy was at work. Michael's older brother and sister did not like having to take him along when they went out with their friends. They got into fights at school when other kids made fun of Michael. "It seemed like they were always in the principal's office, and my parents had to be called to go to school." Robbie was often left to his own devices while the others helped Michael. He was teased by neighborhood kids and had no one to stick up for him, and his parents could not give him the time and attention he needed. They never intended to ignore him but they were overwhelmed. Michael realizes now that his brothers and sister paid a price for having him live at home. "They won't admit it today, but in their childhood they took a back seat to me," he says. "They knew that they were not getting what they were supposed to be getting. They were never neglected, but I now feel that they took a back seat because my parents were trying to figure out ways to keep me at home and to get everything that I needed."

After a few months, it was clear that the situation was untenable. Not only were few services available for Michael; there were also no real supports for parents like Mr. and Mrs. Kennedy. There was a social stigma attached to having a family member with a disability and the unspoken implication was that it was the parents' fault that their child was "handicapped". Most families kept silent about children who were "sent away", or "odd" relatives who disappeared, or delinquents who "left home". Many, if not most, parents, felt incredible guilt, believing that they had done something wrong that had caused their child's condition.[8]

In this climate of fear and stigmatization, it is no surprise that only a few parents of children with disabilities wrote about their experiences. Even then, their stories rarely made it into mainstream publications. The media was alive with stories of antiwar demonstrations, feminist rallies, student uprisings, rapid and controversial scientific research and a sense of doom as the superpowers steadily increased their nuclear arsenals; there was hardly room for tales of individual families' struggles to meet their children's special needs. One of the pioneering articles was written by Pearl S. Buck, a well-known author, who described her daughter Carol as "The Child Who Never Grew" in the May 1950 edition of *Ladies' Home Journal*. Like many parents of special needs children, Buck was ashamed of her daughter's disability and hid her even from close friends for decades before she decided to make Carol's story public. In the article, Buck told how Carol had grown as expected until around the age of four, but then began to fall behind. When Buck raised her concerns with doctors, she was first advised to wait, as her daughter would eventually outgrow her slow start. Soon it became clear that Carol was not improving, but none of the professionals Buck consulted had any idea how to help her. Buck "remembered a doctor telling her: 'I tell you Madam, the child can never be normal. Do not deceive yourself. You will wear out your life and beggar your family unless you give up hope and face the truth…Find a place where she can be happy and leave her there and live your own life.'"[9] Discussions like these convinced Buck that it was best for her daughter to be among other people who were like her; "her own kind." As a result, Buck sent Carol to live in an institution, the Vineland Training School, where she lived for more than sixty years.[10]

After Buck's publications, one or two other parents wrote their stories, echoing her conviction that institutionalizing children with disabilities was good for the entire family. These stories focused not on the children and their needs, but on the needs of the parents: if they chose to care for their children at home, their marriages would flounder, their other children would suffer, their financial security would be jeopardized and they would not be able to move on with their own lives.[11] Unfortunately, these dire predictions too often reflected cold reality, as the Kennedys were finding out.

One alternative to this gloomy message was a short book written by Dale Evans, wife of the cowboy movie star, Roy Rogers. Their daughter Robin had been born with Down's syndrome and had died at the age of two. Using Robin's voice as the story's narrator, Evans told how parents must find meaning, a purpose, for themselves in the life of their disabled child. It was a message of hope, not despair.[12] Still, it offered little in the way of concrete advice for parents seeking services for their children with disabilities.

These parent narratives were published in the 1950s, long before Michael Joseph Kennedy arrived on the scene. Even if they had been more contemporary, it is still unlikely that Mr. and Mrs. Kennedy would have seen them. The Kennedys did not subscribe to such magazines; they rarely had time to read newspapers and their small black and white TV was usually tuned to children's shows like Mickey Mouse or Captain Kangaroo. Like most people, and certainly parents of disabled children, they sought advice from professionals, not popular literature. In Michael's case, the only professional available was the local doctor.

Michael's parents believed they had nowhere to turn for help with caring for him at home, so again they asked the doctor for advice. This time, he recommended having Michael admitted permanently to the Rome State School, in Rome, New York. Mrs. Kennedy recalls how the doctor described Rome State School in positive terms. He reassured her that Michael would get physical therapy every day. She knew she was doing the best she could, but she would never be able to provide Michael with as much therapy as the doctor said he would receive at Rome State School. Even more important for Mrs. Kennedy, however, was the promise of formal education: he would be living at a State School. Michael was now nine years old and his schooling had been mediocre at best. Mrs. Kennedy was convinced that in order for Michael to succeed as an adult, he would need a solid education. In many ways, Rome State School seemed to offer Michael many opportunities she could never give him if she kept him at home. "It was what the doctor had recommended," she added.

Like most parents, the Kennedys trusted the professional wisdom and counsel of their doctor. They had no reason not to, and there was no one to contradict his advice or offer other recommendations.

Today, the idea of sending a nine-year-old child away to live in an institution seems horrible and cold, but for Mrs. Kennedy, there was no other choice: she wanted Michael to be able to eat, walk, and get educated – in short, to have a future. Over and over again, she recalled her steadfast desire that Michael get both the therapy and the education that she could not provide for him at home. She and her husband also realized they had to make this decision not just for Michael, but also for the whole family. Later, Mr. and Mrs. Kennedy learned of the horrific conditions that Michael and other residents had to endure, but at the time, they believed they were making the best decision for Michael.

Mrs. Kennedy says she thought then, and still believes now, that sending Michael to Rome was a good decision. Michael, however, believed his mother still harbored some guilt. He thought she regretted her decision to send him to each of these institutions, and especially to Rome State School. Asked whether Michael's perception was true, Mrs. Kennedy sat quietly for only a brief moment before answering. "No. No, I don't feel guilty. I did what I had to do. I wanted Michael to have the therapy. I couldn't do that for him. I tried, but he needed more than what I could do. I wanted him to go to school, too. He could get that at Rome. It was better than nothing." She explained that she did not know what kind of schooling Michael would get otherwise, but she was afraid he would get none. Her great hope – her only hope – for Michael's future lay in the possibility of getting him an education, because she was sure he would need knowledge to survive.

Once again, the family packed up Michael's belongings and headed to Rome State School. Michael was not yet ten years old. He took his clothes, his beloved stereo, and his favorite toys. Unlike his previous trips to West Haverstraw and the Shriner's hospital, this time Michael Joseph Kennedy was not going to return home later. His life was going to change forever.

2

The Early Years in Rome

"Very few insane are cured or Feeble minded benefitted by the institutions, not because it was not possible but by the way they are managed by the Public. God help the defectives of the land as man is failing to make much effort."

~ Charles Wilbur, Clerk for the Wilbur Home and School of the Feeble Minded, 1909[13]

Institutionalization of people with disabilities had already been accepted medical practice for a century when Michael was placed at the Rome State School. People with disabilities were traditionally seen as "unfit" and therefore burdens to society, and when the ideas of social Darwinism and eugenics gained popularity in the late 19th century, many Americans came to believe that dependence on public charity was an inheritable trait. Large, residential institutions for everyone who depended on public assistance seemed like an ideal way to minimize the costs of this "burden" and isolate people with disabilities (ranging from physical disabilities and developmental delays to insanity, poverty and alleged promiscuity) from the rest of the population. Consequently, the early part of the twentieth century saw the growth of many residential facilities for people with disabilities or other problems. Initially, these large institutions were meant to restore the "unfit" person's sense of worth through hard work, fresh air and wholesome, routine activities away from the harmful and judgmental gaze of society. Under these bucolic conditions, it was believed, a person could relax, reform his or her ways, and contribute to society through honest work within the confines of the institution. At the same time, such residential facilities ensured that people with disabilities would be kept apart from mainstream society, which was an important concern in an age where most disabilities, mental health problems and immoral or asocial behavior were assumed to be transferable to other members of society, whether by inheritance or by simple proximity. Very few people were sent to these institutions by choice and even fewer had any hope of being deemed fit to leave the institution again.

The institution that was later to become Michael's residence opened in 1894 as the Rome State Custodial Asylum for Unteachable Idiots. Its residents, tellingly called "inmates" at the time, were people from all over New York State who were deemed 'unfit' for society in some way. Some had obvious physical or mental disabilities but many others did not. Orphans, children with behavior problems or possible developmental delays and babies who were not thriving made up a substantial portion of the institution's younger population. Unwed mothers also frequently ended up in institutions like the one in Rome, as women who became pregnant out of wedlock were commonly regarded as promiscuous and likely to dilute the gene pool with inferior moral characteristics. Many residents were simply suffering from conditions resulting from extreme poverty, such as malnutrition or vitamin deficiencies, while others were amputees or victims of accidents. Still, the common denominator for state officials was their need for "custodial" care in a closed institution where they could be isolated from society.

The asylum's mandate was to provide basic care for its residents at the lowest possible cost, which is why the original four buildings were surrounded by 1,200 acres of farmland; although the residents were supposedly "unteachable", it was hoped that many could be put to work in the fields to make the institution largely self-sufficient. Before the turn of the century, this hope was mainly used to justify chronic underfunding, resulting in deplorable conditions for both staff and residents in the institution's first decade. The rooms were damp and poorly ventilated, the plumbing was ancient and there was a serious shortage of furniture.[14] Staff members often worked 15-hour days for subsistence wages. Residents received little training and production on the institution's grounds was disorganized and inefficient. The failure of institutions like Rome to achieve any measure of economic self-sufficiency appeared to justify the common public assumption that their only goal could be to meet inmates' most basic needs for food and shelter.

Conditions improved markedly under the guidance of Superintendent Charles Bernstein, who took charge of the Rome Asylum in 1903. He believed strongly that "housing, clothing and feeding [inmates], and that alone, was surely a short-sighted policy, as under such treatment, they are bound to grow more dull, stupid, destructive, filthy or violent (this depending on treatment) and require a constantly increasing amount of personal attention from the attendants."[15] In other words, following a "custodial" model that focused on providing minimal care for residents was self-defeating as well as economically inefficient, in his view. During Bernstein's long tenure as superintendent, emphasis was placed on work - on the farm, on the wards, in the kitchens and laundries, and later in workshops - and residents were classified not according to their disability, but by their skills and capabilities. The guiding principles of the institution, called "Moral Treatment", were that inmates were to be dealt with kindly, never abused, and restrained only when there was no other way to prevent harm to themselves or others. They were also to be employed whenever and however possible, in order to enhance their value for the institution and prevent negative behavior resulting from boredom.

Under Bernstein's new regime, residents who were strong and able to work were apprenticed early with attendants, learning skills that were equal to those of the paid employees. Inmates who gained expertise passed on skills to their fellows. Men were commonly trained as laborers, doing field work, caring for livestock, making furniture or working in construction. Women learned domestic skills such as cooking, cleaning, childcare and sewing. These occupations were chosen according to the staff's assessment of inmates' capabilities, but also according to demand; Bernstein ensured that inmates could produce marketable goods and provide services that were needed at the institution and in the community. Not only did residents produce goods ranging from canned food to wicker chairs; they also made most of their own clothing, bedding and food, provided a substantial amount of personal care, and even ran the telephone switchboard.[16]

Bernstein also believed that many inmates were educable and the institution's name was accordingly changed to Rome State School in 1919. Children under the age of fourteen and thought to be capable of learning attended school on site. Some were taught to read, write and do sums, but most learned vocational skills such as how to tend gardens, launder rags on a washboard, or punch holes in leather. As students grew older, they were trained for specific jobs needed at the institution. "Domestic training" involved chores such as making beds, cleaning and mopping floors, and personal care of residents known as "low grades" - in other words, those who were unable to care for themselves. In the classroom, "object lessons" showed students miniaturized replicas of real buildings in the community in an effort to teach functional skills. Students even practiced financial transactions with pretend money, although none was given an opportunity to accumulate their own cash.

Superintendent Bernstein understood the value of his labor pool and used it to gain the approval of lawmakers and community leaders. Residents whose work was exemplary were loaned out to the community; their wages were paid directly to the facility. In time, Bernstein developed work arrangements called "colonies", where a team of workers would live and reside together in a group off campus. Initially open only to men, these productive communities contributed a great deal to the institution and the local economy. The strong demand for domestic service workers convinced Bernstein to try "colonies" for women as well, although skeptics feared the consequences of allowing "feeble-minded" women off the grounds, where they would come into contact with men. The women's colonies proved a success, however, paving the way for colonies with more diverse functions, ranging from forestry to textile production, all of which contributed financially to the institution.

Without this "free" labor, the institution would have been cost-prohibitive. With it, however, Bernstein was able to expand both its services and its amenities. Recreational activities were provided on site, and citizens from the Rome area came to enjoy concerts, sporting events and dances, all held on the grounds. The institution even had its own newspaper. The paid staff often came from the area and ended up dedicating their lives to the place, living there year-round. Naturally, families from the area knew each other, and often relatives worked side by side even if only one was an inmate. Charles Bernstein won admiration from other superintendents for his brilliant employment of residents and financial management, and his approach, known as "The Rome Plan", was soon being copied at institutions across the country.

The Rome Plan allowed the School to combine the goals of moral treatment and cost-efficiency, but by the 1920s, the population of residents was increasing at a rate that was neither functional nor sustainable. Bernstein reacted by implementing another idea that took hold: parole. He was convinced that many people committed to Rome's care were perfectly capable of living in the community, especially if their disabilities were physical in nature or largely the result of poor upbringing or poverty. It seemed reasonable for "deserving" inmates to be released from care if they showed themselves to be good workers who posed no threat or burden to society. Candidates for parole were permitted to save money from their wages and were allowed more autonomy to prove their ability to handle independence. Still, parolees had to have an outside sponsor, often a relative or employer, and they were encouraged to maintain frequent contact with the institution and its staff.

In many ways, Rome State School under Bernstein's leadership sounds like a model institution - and in many ways, it was. The inmates were still inmates, though, and many aspects of their lives were controlled and regulated. Work schedules were long and full, designed to keep people fully occupied from breakfast until bedtime, and staff, not residents, decided who performed which tasks. Only selected "higher-grade" workers who lived in colonies were allowed to keep any of the money they earned and most workers never received any form of compensation beyond new clothes. Men and women were segregated by cottage or ward with limited opportunities for mingling. Privacy was difficult to come by, and marriage and family were only possible for attendants or parolees outside the walls of the institution. Although the staff kept meticulous records, it is telling that there are few details of the intimate lives of inmates except for reports of abuse.

The benefits of the "Rome Plan" were also largely reserved for the inmates deemed capable of work, most of whom would not be considered disabled today. For those rated as "low-grades" – in other words, people who needed help with basic tasks like eating, dressing or washing and were not believed capable of taking on "productive" tasks – training was minimal, control was strict and the chance of leaving the institution in any capacity was non-existent. Even inmates whose families petitioned to take them back were routinely denied parole if they were "low-grade", since Bernstein and his staff feared that residents who were not truly productive would harm the institution's reputation if allowed to live in the community. A common punishment for "higher-grade" inmates who misbehaved was to be seated at a "low-grade" table in the dining hall, reinforcing the importance of productivity.[17] In the Rome State School, low-grade also meant low-value.

In the first decades of the 20th century, with Bernstein at the helm, the Rome State School gained national prominence for its superintendent's progressive vision and its residents' productivity and self-sufficiency. At the same time, its population grew; by 1916 it already exceeded its official capacity of 1200, housing more than 1,500 adults and children and employing 200 full-time staff. Initially, this growth was intentional, since Bernstein wanted to move inmates to colonies and also to grant more requests for parole, thus opening spaces on the home campus. The number of new admissions rose faster than the number of residents placed in colonies or granted parole, however, and the population exploded when the Depression hit. Families who otherwise might have cared for disabled or troubled relatives at home faced such financial and personal strain that institutionalization seemed the only option, and admission rates soared. By the 1930s, Rome State School was home to more than 3,000 inmates.

The general economic recovery that accompanied the outbreak of World War II did not alleviate the situation; on the contrary, overcrowding continued and the quality of care decreased significantly as attendants joined the armed forces or left for more lucrative jobs in war industries. When Bernstein died in 1942, Rome State School had 3,950 residents, making it one of the largest institutions of its day. The peace brought no relief, as the war had increased the number of disabled people as well, putting more pressure on the School to expand even though the booming postwar economy made it nearly impossible to hire sufficient staff. By 1956, the number of residents had risen to 4,958. The School was still ostensibly dedicated to helping and training people with disabilities with the goal of restoring at least some individuals to their communities. However, as wards began to overflow, the School changed from a self-sufficient school to a large institution, and then to a larger congregate care facility where it was ever harder to achieve the original ideals of moral treatment and education.

Overcrowding brought many other problems as well. At times, residents had to share beds and personal items. The resulting unhygienic conditions made it easy for disease to spread among residents as well as staff, which stretched attendants to their limits. Little time could be spent on individual care, especially since chronic understaffing required most attendants to work overtime as a matter of routine. To make things worse, in the postwar period courts began ordering juvenile offenders with supposedly "feeble minds" to Rome, changing the dynamics of residential life considerably. In order to cope with these conditions, Rome State School had to focus on the absolute essentials, as simply ensuring that residents were provided with the most basic necessities was already a challenge. The only way to handle the situation was to institute strict schedules and rational procedures that maximized staff efficiency. As a result, all personal care became routinized and attendants focused on controlling and managing residents rather than upholding the tenets of moral treatment, productivity and education. By the 1960s, the Rome State School had, in many respects, come full circle: just like in the 1890s, the institution's primary concern was to meet the most basic needs of its residents as cheaply as possible.

In his first report to the state authorities after becoming superintendent in 1903, Bernstein had complained that this approach - focusing solely on providing minimal care rather than encouraging development and productivity - resulted in inmates "who must necessarily live like animals".[18] Despite Bernstein's efforts to the contrary, this is the situation Michael encountered when his parents dropped him off at the Rome State School in the late 1960s.

Michael was nine years old when he was placed at the Rome State School. He believed then that he was only going to stay there for about six months to relieve some of the strain on his family. He gamely put on a brave face and tried to be on his best behavior with the staff and residents. He mostly remembers crying himself to sleep, unsure where he was or when he would be reunited with his parents. It was a far cry from the busy family life he had been used to at home, with grandmothers, cousins, three siblings and other extended family members all coming and going from his small apartment.

Official records written by the social workers responsible for Michael's admission describe his family as lower class, with veiled references to alcoholism, mental breakdowns and his parents' intermittent work histories. The underlying tone is that Michael was better off in the institution. Michael's parents received very little information about Michael's situation or progress, even when they asked specific questions. According to Michael, "There was a lot of stuff that [my mother] wanted answers to, and she didn't get the answers." Nevertheless, she remained confident that Rome could offer Michael a future that she could not if she kept him at home.

The reports written by the physicians and psychiatrists who initially evaluated Michael describe Michael as a "bright young boy" and "not mentally retarded". These records confirmed Mrs. Kennedy's conviction that he would benefit from a formal education. Over time, however, "mild mental retardation" appeared in

Michael's records, as if this condition developed while Michael was institutionalized. Sadly, it was not unusual for individuals to develop problems in the institution that they never had prior to admission. This pattern is particularly evident among people institutionalized as children, as the institutional setting offers little chance to develop meaningful emotional attachments and rarely provides a rich educational experience. The environment and pattern of institutionalization actually makes for a life of deprivation that is not conducive to intellectual development.

Michael's recollections of his childhood in Rome confirm this pattern and help to explain why his intelligence was less apparent in later records. Although his parents had opted for Rome in part to give Michael access to education, in fact, the institution had little to offer. At the time, it was widely believed that children with disabilities - including adults who were still considered "forever children" mentally - could not benefit much from education. Trying to teach people whose bodies looked and moved so strangely was viewed as a waste of time and money; even if they could learn something, they had no hope of pursuing a "real" career. Professionals classified people with disabilities as "trainables" or "educables". The first group, commonly referred to as TMRs - Trainable Mentally Retarded - could potentially learn to do menial tasks such as sorting, cleaning, farm work or manual labor. In other words, they fit into Bernstein's "higher grades" but would not have been considered for colony life or parole in Bernstein's system. The second group - "educable mentally retarded" or EMRs - were seen as capable of learning some basic skills, including rudimentary reading and/or math. They might work in jobs that required some independence and responsibility, such as messengers or shop assistants.

In both cases, however, physical ability played a key role in assessment, since it was generally assumed that anyone with physical limitations from birth was also very likely mentally retarded. Although initial reports suggested that Michael was intelligent, it is unlikely that anyone at Rome knew how to evaluate his abilities since he could not hold a pencil. He would never have been classified as "educable" because of his physical limitations. The anomaly for Michael, and ultimately, his salvation, was the fact that he could talk fairly clearly. Unlike many of his fellow residents, Michael could speak out.

Rome State School did have an in-house educational program, which Michael attended during his first few months there. It did not focus on academics, however, and no effort was made to design an appropriate individualized educational plan for Michael. He remembers the in-house school as a huge waste of time and says he "couldn't stand it because you didn't do anything." He says, "I can tell you every character there is on *Sesame Street* because that's basically what the morning was, and the other half of the morning you put pegs in a pegboard and then you [went] to lunch, and then after that you lay on mats and [took] naps, and then after that you went back to your unit. And that's what you did all day." Although staff did attempt to teach some skills to the students, they focused on training them to perform simple, repetitive tasks - hence the peg board - with the idea that once these were mastered, students could move on to more complex tasks. This approach ignored students' individual needs and abilities, however. For Michael, with his physical limitations, putting pegs into holes required extreme effort, but he could easily have done sums in his head or dictated a story - he was simply never given the chance. Indeed, Michael believes that *Sesame Street* taught the residents more academic skills than any other part of the program.

Without much in the way of school to fill their days, Michael and the other children had very little to do within the confines of the institution. There were few toys and those that were available tended to be simple ones, without moving parts or complex action. Many toys were broken or simply disappeared after a few days. A television mounted in the corner of the room was supposed to provide entertainment, but it was usually tuned to shows the staff wanted to watch. Michael noted, "The staff would lock up the TV so you could never touch it. We never really watched the news or children's shows." Essentially, the institution had returned to the kind of custodial care it had provided in the 1890s - the kind of care Bernstein had so roundly criticized.

There were also few opportunities to leave the grounds or learn about what was happening in the outside world. When Michael first arrived at Rome State School, the staff told his parents not to visit for at least the first six months, in order to give Michael time to adjust to his new home. Even after that, Michael's family was discouraged from visiting, ostensibly because it was too disruptive for Michael. When Michael's mother asked why she could not see her son, the staff said, "He cries every time you leave", suggesting that isolation from his family was in Michael's best interest. Michael's only opportunity to leave the institution's grounds came when staff decided to take him on a "field trip" to a pumpkin farm or another local attraction. These trips, according to Michael, were "few and far between." Slightly more frequently, Michael was allowed to participate in "community integration" activities ostensibly aimed at familiarizing Rome's residents with "normal" society. Michael says a much more accurate term for these outings is a 'drive-by-sighting'. Staff "would put everyone in a van and drive down to the McDonalds and they would get a coffee, and they would call it 'community integration'! And that is what they would write it up as! I don't call that community integration, I call that a drive-by sighting, because we all stayed in the van and just got to see."

Despite Rome's alleged commitment to community integration, for Michael it was clear that residents were supposed to be sheltered. Since there were no newspapers and the televisions were rarely tuned to news programs, he had no way to keep abreast of current events. Some staff, in particular a favorite person of Michael's named Dave, would let the residents know what was going on in the outside world. Michael recalls Dave's efforts to inform him. "I was left on my own, and I would ask Dave about these things going on, and he would show me what was going on from the news. And of course he had to do it on the sly, you know, because if they found out that he was helping me and teaching me, he would have gotten canned. I had another friend who was a volunteer, and he used to hang out with me, and he used to tell me bits and pieces of what was going on. He would ask if I had heard on the news today about this happening, or that happening. I got my information second and third hand, I never heard it right away."

The overwhelming message that the institution sent to its residents was that they were not people; they did not count as individuals. This message was never stated outright, but it was clear to everyone in the institution. Although the official regulations specified that residents were to be treated humanely and respectfully, the unwritten rules placed the residents completely at the mercy of staff. Kindness was clearly equated with inefficiency, leaving staff little incentive to treat residents well and offering bullies ample leverage to keep potential dissenters quiet. The institution's main goal of custodial care reinforced this unwritten policy of depersonalization. There was no reason to treat Michael and his fellow residents as individuals; indeed, the focus on efficiency that chronic understaffing required made it costly to do so. Michael says, "I distinctly remember on one of the units they had over 50 people living there with only 4 attendants for staff. And I was the only verbal one there at the time. I'll never forget it."

The focus on efficiency invited abuse as well. The laundry system in the institution illustrates this problem poignantly. When Michael moved in, he brought a suitcase with clothes and a few toys from home. His family naturally assumed that he would have some safe place to keep personal items on his unit. Within a short period of time, however, his personal possessions disappeared and his own clothing was mixed in with the generic clothes everyone wore. "Well, I had clothes to wear from home, [my parents] sent me clothes, but I was lucky if I wore them two times in a row. [...] Even though I had stuff, I didn't have it for very long."

One of the reasons why residents rarely wore their own clothes was the main laundry facility at Rome Developmental Center. The laundry room operated all hours of the day and night. To launder clothing for thousands of residents efficiently, all the clothes were washed and dried together. Clean laundry was typically sorted by size and cut, not by owner. Michael's mother "even tried marking my clothes and it didn't make a difference. She would sew my initials on the collars, and my grandmother helped too, sewing my name on the waistband of my pants, and the [staff] would just cut it off. They took scissors and actually cut out the sewing. So I just basically told her to stop buying stuff and taking it [to the institution]." The staff's priority was to be able to dress and undress residents as quickly and easily as possible, so they often chose extra-large garments, regardless of whom they belonged to. Michael recalls, "If you picked me up, my pants would fall down around my ankles!" This was convenient for staff, saving them a step in the undressing process, but embarrassing and degrading for Michael.

The fact that Michael wore pants at all was already something special, as many residents never wore regular clothes in the institution. Instead, they were dressed in one-piece "jump suits". According to Michael, "they came in two colors: one was a dark pea green, and the other one was grey, or sort of tan. [...] They were supposed to snap up on the front, but [staff] put them on backwards so people couldn't take them off. And it was a one-piece jumper. They were made out of that heavy-duty material that you make laundry bags out of, that cotton stuff. Or what the military makes backpacks out of." Another "benefit" of the institutional jumpsuits, from the perspective of the staff, was that they could be used to restrain residents. Michael described how "they would take the tie from the chair, and loop it through the armholes and the back, and then tie it to the chairs so you couldn't move or take it off!" In other words, residents' comfort was not considered; staff comfort and convenience was the determining factor in personal care decisions.

The only times Michael wore nice clothing were the rare occasions he was allowed to visit his family, usually on holidays. People without family outside the institution rarely had regular clothing at all, but those whose families occasionally visited were dressed in regular clothes more frequently. Michael could distinguish residents who had family "outside" from those who did not simply by looking at how they were dressed. "Well, to me, the people who got to go home, some of them were real high-class people. You know what I mean. [Staff] tended to treat them better, and the ones who didn't have family, they just sort of let them be off by themselves. I mean, they worked with them and all, but they didn't treat them with any dignity. [The staff] weren't like, 'You aren't like these people over here, these 12 people with families,' but they just made sure they were dressed up better, and the others had uniforms."

Even when Michael was dressed up for a home visit, he rarely got to wear his own things. He told how "they sent me home one time on a visit with clothes that were three times my size, and my Mother — I wouldn't say she went ballistic — but she was very concerned about where all the stuff that they bought me for birthdays, Christmas, and my confirmation went. They bought me some nice jeans, and shirts, and sweaters, and things, and half the stuff they bought would never come home with me. So she ended up doing what most divorced people do, having one set of clothes with your mother, and one set in Dad's home" – only in Michael's case, he had a set of Rome clothes and a set of home clothes.

Clothing did not just disappear in the facility laundry, though; staff routinely helped themselves to items they found appealing. Michael says that staff members did not even try to hide the fact that they were stealing residents' clothes: "I actually heard someone in Rome once say, 'Oh, my son would like this!' and she just picked it up and walked out the door with it." No wonder he thought "it was like wasting money having your own things."

As if being dressed in shapeless uniforms or ill-fitting, mismatched clothes was not degrading enough, residents were also routinely labeled: "either your name or your number was painted on your skin [with] big markers or a black paint that wouldn't come off," Michael remembers. This way staff "didn't have to ask you your name because they [could] lift up the back of your nightgown." Of course, staff did not want to publicize the fact that they labeled the people under their care in much the same way that the Nazis had tattooed prisoners in Auschwitz, so "if they knew you were going home, they had a wire brush to scrub that stuff off. It would scrape the stuff off. And when you use a wire brush on your skin it is going to rip the skin off, too. And it hurt." The fact that this procedure was excruciating was quite clear to the staff, who also employed it as a punishment for residents who misbehaved, even when no home visit was scheduled. In fact, removing the identification marks was usually even more painful in this case, as the staff had no reason to avoid leaving telltale wounds on residents who were not leaving the grounds.

This is, unfortunately, only one of Michael's many stories of abuse in the institution. Physical punishment for "unacceptable" behavior was the norm, and the definition of "unacceptable" was both fluid and subjective. Staff knew that they could get away with beating residents as long as they did not do permanent damage that could not be explained away with stories of accidents, since most of the people on Michael's unit could neither talk nor get around on their own. Michael was beaten on numerous occasions, just like most of the other people on his unit. "When they didn't want to leave marks, they would put soap in a sock, they covered the soap, and they would smack you as hard as they could." Staff could also move residents at will. "Rome was a huge campus, [and] every building was identified after a letter in the alphabet. And 'I' building was the isolation, lockup building. I spent at least two months in the lockup unit as punishment for running away. But before I got there, I took some severe beatings."

Not surprisingly, Michael was not the only resident who tried to run away. He remembers, "back then if you were gone for 72 hours or whatever it was, you were free. They didn't look for you anymore." This fact, of course, made the prospect of escape very tempting. Although most runaways were quickly apprehended, Michael knew a couple of residents who actually succeeded in getting out of the institution and hiding long enough that the search for them was called off. He stayed in touch with one of them, Jeff.[19] Jeff had been placed in the institution shortly before Michael and was one of the more mobile residents. Michael recalls how "they were short-staffed on one of the units, so they would tell [Jeff] to watch the other people." Although staff trusted Jeff with this responsibility, it did not stop them from "beat[ing] the heck out of him, too." Jeff got fed up and started looking for opportunities to break out. Michael tells the story like this: "At one time there was this new staff [member] and it was his turn to put out the garbage. So Jeff said, 'I'll take the garbage out for you.' So the new guy didn't know [the rules] and he unlocked the door. So Jeff says he will take out the garbage, and he goes and hides near the cans, and then hops on a city bus for a dollar that takes him downtown. When he gets on the city bus he crouches down behind the seats and they can't see him anymore. He makes it to Utica, and calls his friend, who comes and gets him, and then he stays there with his friend. And now he is free!"

Today, Jeff lives in Utica. His friend helped him to find a job and a place to stay; only after Jeff was settled did the friend inform anyone that Jeff was "ok, and safe." Unlike nearly all of his former buddies, Jeff made a life for himself outside the institution.

Michael and the others had no such luck. They had to make the best of their situation. In order to protect each other, Michael describes a secret code he and the other residents had with each other. Often the code was used to warn one another about a particular staff member. "We had this thing that was like a code. And we had it for certain people, so I learned to read a lot of people's body language. If a certain person walked in a room, all you had to do was watch their body language and you knew. Yeah, we had a pact. [The other residents] couldn't speak, and they didn't have devices to speak, so you had other ways to communicate."

Because he could talk clearly and reasonably fluently, Michael felt he occupied a unique position: he could speak on others' behalf and stick up for them. This did not endear him to the staff, who generally resented his early efforts to advocate for himself and others. Michael's mother tried to make clear to staff that Michael was not the sort of child who reacts to injustice with a stiff upper lip. She told them, "You think he is going to be quiet and all, but if he sees something that he doesn't like, his mouth isn't in his pocket." Michael adds, "I really had to talk because I have seen animals get better treatment than what we got. The reason why I say that is because I saw it with my own eyes. I was one of those people that was pretty loud because I had to tell." He remembers one friend on his unit who could write even though he could not talk. This person wrote, "'Michael we want to speak out on this stuff but we are afraid. We can't cause we are intimidated.' And that's what he wrote. He said he commended me, putting my life on the line."

3

Leaving Rome for Home Sweet Home

Michael continued to speak out, but he also paid the price. One time he saw how staff were torturing another child with a cattle prod. They called it "shock treatment" and seemed to be getting a kick out of watching the child recoil and scream. Michael was used to enduring abuse and seeing his friends humiliated, but this was more than he could stand. Knowing he was powerless to stop the staff members from hurting his friend, he sneaked off the unit and told one of the administrators what was going on. It was impossible for the administrator to ignore such an egregious case of abuse and the staff received a reprimand. Michael was punished much more severely for his courage: the staff simply stopped giving him his meals. When the food service staff asked why Michael was not eating, the staff on his unit said he was not feeling well and had refused to take any food. For more than two weeks, Michael got no regular meals.

Luckily for Michael, his father stopped by to visit and realized something was wrong. He asked Michael what was up, but because there were staff members within earshot, Michael said he would tell his father everything later. Before he left, Michael's father gave him a model to put together so he could improve his dexterity and promised to come back in a few days. As soon as he was gone, the staff on Michael's unit started making subtle threats about how they would get him back another way for turning them in to the administrator. He soon found out what they had in mind.

From then on, every time Michael took out his new model and put it together, as soon as he was done one of the other residents came up, took the model away and ripped it apart. The staff did not reprimand the other boy at all; instead, they bought him a soda as a reward. Michael ignored them and painstakingly put his model back together again. Again the boy came and ripped it apart, and received another soda from the staff. Michael was livid – as he says, "I'm Irish and French, two tempers don't just fit together" – but he knew the boy was only tormenting him because the staff was encouraging him. He put the model away, but the next time he took it out, the same thing happened. Finally, after the fourth time the other boy had destroyed his work and been rewarded with a soda, Michael spoke directly to one of women on the staff. He said, "if he does it again, I'm going to smack him," but the woman did not react even though it was clear that she had heard. True to his word, Michael backhanded the other resident when he tried to "earn" his fifth soda. "I hit him so hard I knocked him out of his chair, ass over teakettle!" Michael recalls. "I didn't intend to hit him so hard that he would fall."

Now the staff had an excuse to punish Michael openly, as he had clearly broken a rule. Their punishment also broke numerous laws, though: they fetched a rope, tied it around Michael's ankles and hoisted him up so he was hanging upside down from the lintel of one of the ward's oversized doorways. They were preparing to have more 'fun' when Michael's father arrived with Michael's older brother, Kevin, and his uncle. Although he was terrified and in horrible pain, Michael remembers how cool his father appeared at that moment. "My father went over very nonchalantly and took me off the door. He had to cut the rope off. It was so tight you couldn't untie it." As soon as he had settled his son back in his wheelchair, Mr. Kennedy demanded to see the director. When the staff did not respond to this request, Mr. Kennedy marched to the director's office and knocked on the door. The director tried to put him off, calling from behind the closed door that he was too busy, but Mr. Kennedy was not willing to wait. He kicked the door in and confronted the director, who was "busy" smoking a cigar with his feet up on the desk. Mr. Kennedy demanded to know why Michael had been hung by his feet from a doorframe and the director responded that the staff had deemed it a necessary response to Michael's act of violence toward another resident. He admitted that the other child had not been punished for repeatedly destroying Michael's model, and when Mr. Kennedy asked what the director planned to do to remedy the situation the director informed him that "it was none of his damn business."

This was the last straw. Michael remembers the ensuing conversation vividly. "My father reached over the desk and grabbed the guy by the neck. Dad said, 'Now you're going to answer me or I'm going to bounce you off every wall in this room, including the window. You better give me what I want to know.' The director said, 'Try it.' That's the wrong thing to say to my father when he's pissed off. He really did bounce him off a few walls. And he said, 'now are you going to tell me or am I going to do this again — even harder?'" In the end, Mr. Kennedy realized that the director was never going to admit that his staff had behaved inappropriately, nor would he take steps to improve conditions in the institution. Even worse, he knew Michael would suffer the minute he was left alone on his unit. He saw no alternative but to take him home.

Michael later discovered that the director did initiate disciplinary proceedings against the staff members who had abused him and most lost their jobs, although one was reinstated after a short time. The director also pressed charges against Michael's father, though, and Mr. Kennedy ended up in jail for a short period of time for defending his son against the people who were supposed to be caring for him. No one apologized to Michael for the inhumane way he had been treated.

Although memories of the incident continued to haunt him, the outcome was a dream come true for Michael. It was wonderful to live at home with his parents and siblings again. Michael's parents both worked at the Smith Corona typewriter plant in Cortland, NY. They lived in one of the ground floor apartments in a big old house in the neighboring town of Homer. It was a bit cramped for two adults and four teenagers, but Michael loved the place.

"We were right on the water, the river, and we had these big old trees and stuff. And we could walk around, and go places in town. We were really free. And we had all this space! My sister was older than me, but my brothers were about the same age as me, and they took me around, riding bikes and stuff. I remember the bridge at the back of house, in our backyard. You could drive over it and there was a river right there." Giggling at the thought, Michael continued, "my younger brother, he was in this chemistry class, and he needed a chemistry set for class, 'cause they were doing all these chemistry experiments. So my parents bought him this chemistry set, and [laughing hard at this memory] he had this friend named Zack or something, and they were on the back porch, mixing these concoctions and stuff and they, [more laughing] and they blew up the porch!! They blew off the back of the porch! All I heard was this big KABOOM! And the next thing you know, there was all this black smoke and I was cracking up. And they said, 'If you tell Mom…' and then Mom said, 'I know what we are doing: we are taking the chemistry set away from you!' It was so funny! I think Mom was downstairs in the laundry, or cooking in the kitchen, or doing something, and the next thing you know, there is this big explosion! And the back porch is smoking!"

For the first time in many years, Michael had a taste of living with his family for an extended period of time. It felt good. He still needed a lot of help with his eating, dressing, and personal care, though. "I knew it was a lot to ask, caring for me, I knew that," he now recalls. His mother had been the main caregiver when he was younger and every time he was home for holiday visits. This time, Michael's sister and two teenaged brothers needed to pitch in and help out. Michael's father saw that his wife could not work full-time at the factory, manage the housework and take over all the tasks Michael could not accomplish alone. Michael is certain his father told his brothers in particular that they had to take responsibility for the bulk of Michael's care, even though neither brother will admit it today. His sister helped as well; according to Michael, "she was always good at the hands-on stuff." Michael's father tried to help, too, but especially after he started his own trucking business he was away too much to offer reliable help. The physical aspect of Michael's personal care was often too much for him when he was there. "My father was never good with the hands-on stuff. He admitted this once, and I think that is why he instituted that they, my siblings, had to help. He knew my mother needed help."

At first, the arrangement worked well and Michael's brothers included him in many of their daily activities. Michael remembers that "I didn't have any friends to hang out with but my brothers did. They tried their damnedest to make sure I wasn't going to be isolated or anything; they tried their best." Over time, however, they began to resent Michael because his care took up so much of their time. Michael saw their frustration: "they couldn't go and do things with their friends. Nothing against me, but you know they couldn't get away. [...] They never really said anything against me, [...] didn't really complain about it or anything, but they really wanted my parents to know that they shouldn't have to do this stuff."

After a while, Michael's brothers were less willing to take him along when they met their friends and started finding excuses to leave Michael's care to their mother. Michael says "there came a point when they didn't want me palling around with them or anything like that. And I didn't really want to do that either. 'Cause you know, you need your own friends." He remembers how his older brother said "It's not that I don't love him, but I need my own friends, my own space," and Michael could not blame him for wanting that. He just could not do everything that needed to be done on his own, and no one else could help.

Gradually, Michael's mother took over more and more of his care, although it was physically and mentally exhausting for her. His father searched in vain for some alternative. First, he turned to relatives. Although Michael "came from a big family on both sides," he remembers, "there were only four people on each side that would even remotely try to help out, out of the whole slew of them." They were willing to try but had little experience actually taking care of Michael, and organizing a regular schedule proved impossible. When

Michael's parents realized that they could not rely on relatives for help, they tried asking local agencies to send someone to share the workload, but local officials "wouldn't give them the time of day." According to Michael, his parents "literally tried everything they could to keep me. My Dad took time off from work, he even closed his business as a trucker, he stopped driving for a while" but to no avail. The Kennedys could not afford to hire a personal care attendant and they could not take care of Michael alone.

The atmosphere in the Kennedy home was tense as Michael's parents debated what to do. Although they explored every alternative they could think of, it seemed that the only viable option was to send Michael back to Rome. Michael remembers how upset his parents were, especially his father. "It was painful for me, but it was also painful for them. They didn't want to do it. Before they made the decision to call the social worker to send me back, my father was up, night after night, tossing and turning around in his head, and all you could see was his moods. And they actually got into an argument. Dad kept saying, 'I don't care what you do but he is not going back!'"

The Kennedys invited their relatives to a family meeting to discuss options for Michael. With heavy hearts, they decided together that Rome was the only solution. They knew conditions there had been horrible but they hoped things had improved in the time Michael was at home, and they saw clearly that they could not continue to keep him with them. Michael was devastated when he realized what was happening. "I was angry 'cause I thought it was me who did something, but I didn't know what. I thought maybe I had said something. But I wasn't the type of kid to be mean or anything. I would say what I felt under no uncertain terms, but I was never mean. But I kept thinking, well, what did I do that I have to be sent back? And I begged them, I begged them not to do it."

After talking it through with his parents, Michael began to understand that his family "had no other choice" but to return him to the institution. "I could also see that they had to; they didn't have the stuff they needed." He had no hope that conditions had improved in his absence; he knew how slowly things changed within the institution's walls. He realized, though, that the situation at home was untenable and he would have to manage as best he could on his own in the institution. He was only fifteen years old.

Looking back, Michael is sure that the decision to return him to Rome essentially broke his parents' hearts. His father could not forgive himself for breaking up his family even though he knew it was impossible for Michael to live at home without more help. Michael says, "I don't think he wanted to live with himself after that. I think that is why he drank. Because he couldn't live with himself. To hide the pain from doing it. 'Cause he thought he failed me again. And that's what he said. He smoked like a fiend. He drank like a fiend when he wasn't working. 'Cause I don't think he could live with himself. And he drank before all this, but it wasn't as intense as after I went back. [...] He just said, 'to hell with it.' He was punishing himself."

Michael's mother also felt guilty for sending her son to Rome a second time. She told Michael "that it was her fault that they put me in there [Rome] in the first place, on account of her nervous breakdown, and now they were doing it all over again." Moreover, this time she knew how much Michael hated it there; the first time, she believed that Rome would offer Michael chances she could not, but this time she had no illusions. She saw how devastating the decision was, not only for Michael, but also for his father, and blamed herself for failing to manage the situation. Michael still fears "she is going to go to her grave feeling awful." He has told her time and again that he knows she had no choice and he does not think she failed him, but she always replies "yes, but that doesn't excuse what I did."

4

"Wait...I'm Going Back? NO!! Not Rome Again!!"

Although Michael understood that his family could not cope with him living at home, as much as they wanted him to be with them, he harbored a secret hope that he would not have to return to the institution in Rome, which was now officially named Rome Developmental Center and called RDC. It was heartbreaking for the whole family to realize that there were no other options for Michael and especially hard for him not to feel abandoned and forlorn. His parents tried to take some comfort from the fact that Michael would get more therapy, but Michael entertained no such hopes. He was sure the institution would be just as "awful" as it always had been. This time, though, he was older and wiser – and prepared for the worst. Rather than resigning himself to his fate, Michael was determined to be even more "feisty" and outspoken than before, regardless of the consequences. He says, "I went back with this huge chip on my shoulder, and I just thought 'to hell with it all; what are they going to do to me now?' I've been there, done that, and I know what it is like. And I still couldn't keep my mouth shut! I felt like I had to be the one to speak up for others still, even if it meant getting into trouble again. Who cares? [...] I had nothing to lose. I made it my job to speak up and not let things pass."

Because he already knew the system and routines, Michael adjusted to life in the institution quickly, if not willingly. He recalls wryly, "the food was still awful, the situation was awful, and I had to make the best of it." He was assigned to Pediatric Building 52, where he quickly established a circle of friends. Even the staff noticed his sense of humor and ability to "[get] along well with everyone."[20] In keeping with the institution's new mission as a "developmental center", the staff also scheduled occupational therapy, recreational therapy, speech therapy and educational services in the "young adult program" for Michael. The occupational therapist suggested better ways to position Michael and included him in a "sensorimotor group [...] designed to give alternatives to the sitting position so that Mike's [sic] musculoskeletal status [would not] deteriorate."[21] The speech therapist worked with him on improving his breath control to make his speech more intelligible. This therapist also set a goal for Michael to "demonstrate an improvement in syntax ability, i.e., 'the way in which words are put together to form phrases, clauses and/or sentences."[22] According to official records, Michael also enjoyed recreational activities like "camping field trips, picnics, movies, arts & crafts, and other ward activities"[23] At least on paper, Michael was finally receiving the services his parents had so badly wanted for him.

The reality was quite different, however. Michael's occupational therapy in the "sensorimotor group" was not actually provided by an occupational therapist, but by untrained staff members on the night shift. Although the therapist recommended that Michael sit less and be positioned in different ways to maintain his muscle tone, no one acted on those recommendations; he still spent the vast majority of his time sitting in his wheelchair or lying down. In fact, there was no pressing need for staff to help Michael or anyone else out of bed if they did not want to, since according to Michael, "we didn't have regular beds; we had metal cribs and they were the big ones. And they were on wheels so they could move you to wherever they needed." Michael's speech therapist was terminated after a few months and no one took his place; instead, the Senior Speech and Hearing specialist "recommended that Michael be encouraged to use proper syntax and breath control during his conversational speech in his other programs."[24] Naturally, no speech therapists were present at these "other programs". Michael does not remember going on any field trips, picnics or cinema visits aside from rare "drive-by sightings" like those he had experienced during his previous stay, nor did he do arts and crafts. The "ward activities" referred to in the report consisted of sitting or lying around and watching television shows chosen by the staff.

The one bright spot in Michael's existence at RDC was school. Soon after he arrived, he discovered that some young residents were allowed to go to school outside the grounds of the institution and he wanted to be one of them. In the fall of 1977, he got his wish when he was selected to attend special education classes at the Kernan School in the city of Utica, which was more than an hour's drive away from Rome. Michael says: "I liked that school because that was the only time that I got off the grounds of the institution."[25] His teacher reported that Michael was "easy to motivate and enjoys challenges presented to him"[26] and his caseworker described him as "very happy" about attending school.[27] Unfortunately, the curriculum was not adapted to meet Michael's unique needs or to build on his strengths. Ostensibly, Michael had a right to a free and appropriate education in the least restrictive environment according to the Education for All Handicapped Children Act (P.L. 94-142), which had been passed in 1975, when Michael was fourteen.[28] The definition of "appropriate" and "least restrictive" were open to interpretation, though, and most schools were still firmly convinced that the most appropriate education for children with disabilities was one where they had no contact with non-disabled peers. In Michael's case the RDC staff already saw the Kernan School as a special opportunity for him. It never occurred to them that with the proper assistance and accommodations, he could attend a regular high school.

Michael's family continued to support him as best they could. His parents brought him home for visits whenever they had time off from work, even if it was just a long weekend, and his father sometimes came to Rome to see him. When the factory Mr. Kennedy worked for shut down, the family moved back to Tupper Lake, where they had strong roots and a number of close relatives. Michael and his parents immediately began to pursue the possibility of having him transferred to Sunmount Developmental Center, a much smaller institution located right in Tupper Lake. Although Sunmount was no more homey or pleasant than Rome, at least it was close enough to make more frequent visits possible. Also, since Sunmount was one of the region's biggest employers, there was a chance that Michael might find familiar, friendly faces among the staff. If nothing else, the staff there would know that Michael had people nearby looking out for him.

Michael's social worker in Rome was willing to permit a transfer, but was convinced that Michael would be better off – and more likely to be offered a placement – at Syracuse Developmental Center. In April 1978, the social worker noted, "Mike and his family are still inclined to feel that transfer to Sunmount is a realistic goal—although I have confronted both parents and Mike with the fact that it is unlikely to be arranged. I have, however, encouraged Mike to visit the center while on leave with his parents over Memorial Day weekend and have shared with Sunmount the fact that they wish to have a tour. Following this visit, I will help Mike to reconsider the advantages of placement in the Syracuse area, especially since his friend [name blacked out] was recently transferred and is happy at Syracuse."[29] Why the social worker suggested a costly and time-consuming trip to Sunmount even though a transfer was "unlikely to be arranged" is a mystery. It is not clear how much the social worker's desire to have Michael placed at Syracuse Developmental Center affected the ultimate decision, but in the end, Michael was not allowed to move to Sunmount.

The rejection of Michael's application to transfer to Sunmount did not reflect any desire to keep him at Rome; on the contrary, Michael had the distinct impression that most of the staff would have loved to see him leave. Because he was not only verbal, but also vocal, Michael presented a threat. "Nobody else could speak, so when they had big visitors they kept me out of view. I was shoved in a back ward somewhere so I couldn't really tell them what was going on," he remembers. He was ready and willing to "scream and yell and all" if there was any chance of his voice being heard, but those chances were few and far between and always entailed an element of risk.

Despite the risk involved, advocacy was desperately needed. The story of Michael's friend Bobby[30] helps to explain why. When they first met, Bobby was one of the few other verbal residents on Michael's unit, although he could not speak as well as Michael. The two boys had a lot in common. Michael remembers that Bobby "had come into the system because his mom and dad split up, and mom just couldn't handle him anymore, kind of like my situation. So they told his mother they had this fine institution, and he wasn't retarded at all." Bobby's behavior during official observations suggested the exact opposite, however. "Every time the reviewers came in to review the books he would be acting all kinds of crazy and when they left I asked him, 'Bobby, why do you act like that?' and he goes, 'Well, when you tell people what is going on in here and they don't listen and pay attention to you, but if you act all crazy and stuff they pay attention!' So if you hoot and holler and stuff, that's when they start to pay attention." This was a lesson Michael took to heart, especially as he grew older and more articulate: he knew he had to speak out loudly "if something just wasn't right."

While Bobby and Michael lived on the same unit, they developed a strong friendship. They came to rely on one another for support and comfort. After a time, though, Bobby was moved to another unit "because he was getting into too much trouble." According to Michael, "the system made him kind of…I don't want to say retarded… but the system made him angry." He was frustrated by the injustice and poor treatment and saw little hope of a better future. Bobby had a hard time on the new unit without Michael to keep his spirits up. Michael visited him every day when he got home from his school program but it was not the same. In desperation, Bobby "went up to one of the staff one time and he said he was depressed. 'Cause he didn't know why things were changing and all and he wanted someone to talk to him. He was real depressed. So [the staff member] said, 'Bobby, why don't you just go and kill yourself?!' Now, mind you, he couldn't do anything by himself, and she told him to go and kill himself.

"One day I went down there when the change of shift was hap-pening, from the day to evenings. I went to open his room and his door was locked. I thought this was kind of weird because he couldn't even lock his door himself. So I waited until the shift changed [...] and after the shift changed, I opened the door, and walked in the room with my chair, and I saw him hanging from the sprinklers, in his room. And there was a note on his nightstand that read, 'Michael I tried to talk to somebody but she told me to go kill myself. So I figured that would be the best thing to do.'"

"So I soon found out that he had convinced another resident who used to live with him to help him commit suicide. He said, 'now tie this sheet around my neck, throw it up over the sprinkler and tie it as tight as you can, and then tie it off. Then when you get ready, yank my chair out from underneath me.' But then I found out he told the guy to lock the door behind him on the way out. So he locked the door.

"So I went out there, and the staff person who told him this, she was supposed to be changing shifts, and she wasn't gone yet. I went over there and I showed her the note he had wrote [sic], and I said, 'Do you realize what you just told this person to do?' She lifted up the note, looked at me and said, 'So? What do you want me to do about it?' And just left it at that. So I said, 'You know what? You are one cold...' And you know what? She got away with it! She said it was my word against hers. She had everyone else on her side, she never was prosecuted or anything, and it was me against all of them. And the real sad thing was that his mother just gave up and never did anything about it. And my Dad used to bring him cake and stuff when he visited me, and guess who had to be the one to tell [Dad] that [Bobby] had hung himself? Me! And my face turned as white as that envelope when I walked in and saw him. And I will never forget that as long as I live. And I am almost 50 years old, and I will never ever forget that. And how someone could be so cold-hearted as to say that to someone...and the system can overlook something like that."

By the time Michael turned 18, life in the institution was clearly beginning to take its toll on him. When he first started school, his teacher noted that "he need[ed] to be encouraged to do more things for himself as most others are inclined to wait on him."[31] Just six months later, the staff on his ward reported, "at this time, it seems Michael is able to do less for himself than he has in the past. He doesn't even show any interest in trying. This may be because it is getting just too much for him or because his friends are always there to do things for him."[32] Michael also noticed how difficult it was for his family to live with the decision to institutionalize him. He recalls, "my Dad still came to visit, but I could tell it was really hard for him. Especially since he was the one who really knew what my life was like [at RDC] before he took me home, and then he had to bring me back. I could tell it killed him. And that's when he seemed to get really old, and I could tell he was drinking a lot." We can only assume that Michael's father saw similar changes in his son. As Michael recalls, "To be honest, to put it plain and simple, I didn't think I had a future because [...] I didn't know if I could find people who were going to help me get out.

In fact, there were people working to help him and all of his fellow residents "get out", – but neither Michael nor his parents knew they existed ... yet.

5

Another Institution - Moving to Syracuse Developmental Center

Although Michael and his parents were not aware of them, fundamental changes in the way New York State handled people with disabilities were in the making. Even before Michael moved to Rome, committed reformers were working to improve conditions in state-run institutions and make more opportunities available to people like Michael. Two landmarks in the fight for disability rights were the Willowbrook Consent Decree, signed in 1975, and Public Law 94-142, known as the Education for all Handicapped Children Act of 1975. Both altered the way Rome Developmental Center and other institutions were run, and helped to bring about the move to close down such large residential facilities to enable people with disabilities to live in the community instead.

Willowbrook was a large institution like the Rome State School, originally built as a hospital on a large parcel of land on Staten Island. It opened just in time to provide care for wounded servicemen during World War II but after the war, the campus was turned over to the New York State Office of Mental Hygiene rather than the Veterans' Administration. In 1951, the Willowbrook State School opened its doors as an institution for children and adolescents with disabilities. Willowbrook's mandate was to care for people considered profoundly mentally retarded, but in reality, many of the residents were placed there simply because their families were unable or unwilling to provide for them. The treatment children received there can hardly be called "care". The institution was chronically overcrowded and services were minimal.[33] The living conditions at Willowbrook were horrendous; later documentation revealed that there were not enough beds, chairs, bathrooms or even clothes for all the residents, with the result that many spent their days sitting on floors covered with dirt and feces, often in the nude. The over-worked, under-supervised staff "resorted to prison-style control tactics: disruptive residents were confined in solitary 'pits' and left for hours or were beaten with keys and sticks."[34]

Doctors responsible for the inmates also used them as guinea pigs for their own research. In one controversial medical study carried out between 1963 and 1966, healthy children were deliberately infected with the virus that causes hepatitis and then monitored to gauge the effects of gamma globulin in combating it. Other studies used unethical methods to test vaccines for childhood diseases and the effects of hormone therapy. In order to have their children admitted to Willowbrook in the first place, parents were required to sign a consent form permitting participation in such experiments, and since most had no other means to care for a child with severe disabilities, most signed. Unscrupulous doctors capitalized on this unusual situation to carry out research that never would have been permitted on other human subjects.

Although a few stories of abuse appeared in the local press earlier, it was not until 1965, when NY State Senator Robert Kennedy made a surprise visit to Willowbrook, that the public was made aware of the horrific living conditions there. In a subsequent statement to the press, Kennedy called Willowbrook a "snake pit" in which he saw people "living in filth and dirt, their clothing in rags, in rooms less comfortable and cheerful than the cages in which we put animals in a zoo."[35] Over the next decade, newspapers reported occasionally on residents who were raped, beaten and even strangled to death.[36] Officials responded with promises of reform, but few actual improvements were made. Then, in early 1972, Geraldo Rivera publicized gruesome scenes from inside the institution's walls in an exposé called "Willowbrook: The Last Disgrace".[37] A public outcry ensued and just three months later the New York Civil Liberties Union filed a class-action lawsuit against the state on behalf of the current residents of Willowbrook, who were designated as the "Willowbrook Class". After three years of litigation, the judge issued a landmark decision, the Willowbrook Consent Decree of 1975.[38]

The Willowbrook Consent Decree determined that the Willowbrook Class and others "similarly situated" – in other words, Michael and people like him – "had a constitutional right, under the Eighth and Fourteenth Amendments, to protection from harm". In a 29-page appendix, it outlined specific procedures for improvement of every aspect of residential life and care at Willowbrook, based on "the recognition that retarded persons, regardless of the degree of handicapping conditions, are capable of physical, intellectual, emotional and social growth, and upon the further recognition that a certain level of affirmative intervention and programming is necessary if that capacity for growth and development is to be preserved, and regression prevented."[39] Another provision was that Willowbrook had to fulfill the requirements laid out in the Decree or close its doors. New York's governor, Hugh Carey, extended the scope of the Decree to include all facilities operated by the State Office of Mental Retardation and Developmental Disabilities (OMRDD), including Rome State School. For Michael, this meant changes were in progress, even if he would not see the outcome for several years.

Around the same time, disability rights activists won another key victory when Congress ratified Public Law 94-142, the Education for all Handicapped Children Act of 1975. Before the law was passed, only about half of America's approximately 8 million children with disabilities were receiving "appropriate educational services which would enable them to have full equality of opportunity" and an estimated 1 million children were not being educated at all.[40] The new law asserted that all children, regardless of disability, had a right to a "free appropriate public education" as well as to related services such as transportation and therapy, all at no cost to their families.[41] In addition, it stipulated that an annual individual education plan (IEP) be designed for each child, laying out the child's present abilities, identifying annual goals and specifying the setting in which they could best be achieved. Whenever possible, this setting should be one in which children without disabilities were also being educated. The program that enabled Michael to attend the Kernan School was instituted as a result of this law; during his previous stay at Rome, there was no requirement that residents be educated.

These two major legal developments had an important impact on the lives of people with disabilities, including Michael. One of the most obvious changes, although hardly the most significant, was that New York's State Schools were renamed "Developmental Centers." Much more importantly, the directors of the Developmental Centers were charged with identifying members of the "Willowbrook Class" and facilitating the process of "repatriation" of developmental center residents back to their home communities. Not every developmental center director took this task to heart, but Thomas Coughlin, director of Syracuse Developmental Center, decided to seek out local experts who were committed to improving the lives of people with disabilities. He found them at the Center on Human Policy.

The Center on Human Policy, an organization affiliated with Syracuse University, was founded in 1971 to bring together experts in the fields of educational and disability policy, research, and advocacy in order to promote the rights of people with disabilities. Syracuse University Dean Burton Blatt, the founder and original director of the Center on Human Policy, was its driving force. His work in the field of disability studies and education established the guiding principles for the emergence of a new social movement known as "deinstitutionalization". He drew on his stature as a scholar and social reformer to attract the finest minds and most dedicated disability rights activists to the Center on Human Policy, where they pursued a common goal of exposing the deplorable conditions in New York's institutions and defining the parameters of disabled children's right to education.

Even before the passage of the Education for all Handicapped Children Act of 1975, the Center on Human Policy sponsored think tanks and invited visiting professors to investigate disability rights. The Center also worked closely with local agencies and organizations such as the Syracuse United Cerebral Palsy Association (now ENABLE) and the local Association for Retarded Citizens (ARC) as well as funding initiatives for community education and the development of model programs. Center publications covered research on everything from legal issues and educational initiatives to the daily life experiences of people with disabilities, and sold posters and T-shirts that offered individuals a means to support deinstitutionalization. The Center on Human Policy was obviously best equipped to take on the daunting task of finding the original members of the Willowbrook Class and figuring out how best to meet their needs, so Tom Coughlin offered to pay the Center for three staff members to take on the job. Douglas Biklen, the Syracuse University professor in charge of hiring at the time, found three disability rights advocates who later made a huge difference in Michael's life: Bernice Schultz, Diane Murphy and Carole Hayes Collier.

Bernice Schultz grew up in a close-knit, activist family where she was encouraged to work for justice and social equality. In the Syracuse area, she was known for fighting discrimination on numerous fronts with the American Civil Liberties Union (ACLU). She jumped at the chance to help serve the cause of social justice at the Center. Recalling her early work, she said her main motivation was "values, values, values, it's still about the right values…the Center on Human Policy knew what their goals were" — and they were goals she shared. She agreed with people at the Center that living in an institution was not normal; institutions, by their very nature, were meant to keep the inmates in and the general public out. The civil rights movement had already demonstrated that separate could not be equal, and Bernice was determined to show that separation could not be normal, either. Helping members of the 'Willowbrook class' to escape institutions seemed like a wonderful way to start.

Diane Murphy was committed to the same goals but she brought a different background to the Center. Diane was pursuing a doctorate in social work in the early 1970s when she was asked to head up one of the Center on Human Policy's joint projects with the Syracuse Legal Services Office. The project involved taking small groups of students from Syracuse University's law school to visit Rome State

School to show them the egregious lack of adequate schooling for the institution's school-age residents and to guide them in preparing arguments for the legal right of all children to receive a public education. Diane did not meet Michael when she toured Rome State School – since the institution staff wanted Diane and her students to see their facility in a positive light, it is likely that they made sure vocal "troublemakers" like Michael were out of the way that day – but her visit made a lasting and horrifying impression on her.

> Everywhere we went, someone had to unlock the doors and relock them behind us. In one room, when the door was opened, we saw children in cages, just lying in their cribs or on the floor. It was a cavernous room and most of the children were half nude. There was a drain in the floor. When we entered everyone turned to stare at us, and then they began slithering across the floor, trying to touch us. When we left and the door was locked behind us, I went into the bushes and threw up.

In subsequent years, she dedicated her professional life to creating alternatives to large institutions so that people with disabilities could live dignified lives in the community.

The last of the trio, Carole Hayes Collier, was the one who first 'found' Michael soon after he moved to Syracuse from Rome.[42] Carole came to the Center from the Syracuse United Cerebral Palsy Association, where she worked closely with – and not just for – people with disabilities like Michael's. A recovering mental patient herself, Carole had been involved in some of the early research on abuses at Willowbrook and had worked as a staff member at a Syracuse mental hospital, so she brought a unique perspective to the task. Together, these three women possessed a combination of skills and experience, coupled with a strong commitment to social justice, that equipped them to make a real difference in the lives of disabled people. The Center on Human Policy gave them the means to make it happen.

As Diane, Bernice and Carole soon found out, it was one thing to identify and locate members of the Willowbrook class – although that was tedious, often frustrating work in itself – and quite another to develop practical living arrangements for them outside of institutions. The Syracuse Chapter of the Association for Retarded Citizens (ARC) was awarded a grant for $300,000 by the U.S. Department of Housing and Urban Development. The New York State Office of Mental Retardation matched the grant with the intent of building three group homes for people with developmental disabilities. Another pioneering organization, Transitional Living Services of Onondaga County, dedicated itself to setting up supervised apartments and other supported housing options for people who wanted to leave the institution. At the same time, administrators in the institutions also made efforts to comply with the stipulations of the Willowbrook Consent Decree so that residents were treated with more dignity and respect. Although the process of deinstitutionalization was fraught with problems, frustration and false starts, the tide was clearly turning in favor of valuing people with disabilities as members of the larger community, and Michael was poised to play a key role in ensuring that their voices were heard.

6

More new beginnings

"What would man be without Utopia? He must aim at the unattainable in order to realize the attainable and to make one step forward."

~ Thomas Mann

The momentous changes that resulted from the Willowbrook Consent Decree made a difference in Michael's life, minimally at first, but more and more as time progressed. For one thing, he became a resident of Rome Developmental Center overnight, although his address did not change. More importantly, the cooperative agreement that allowed Michael to attend classes at the Kernan School was a direct result of the RDC's efforts to comply with the terms of the Consent Decree. Similarly, his social worker's willingness to help Michael transfer – even though she ignored his wishes and those of his family in the process – was surely motivated by a desire to show RDC's progress toward realizing the goals set forth in the Consent Decree.[43] Although Michael did not really want to move to Syracuse, which was substantially further away from his family's home than Rome, in the end it turned out to be a turning point in his life.

As Michael remembers it, August 9, 1978 began just like any other day at Rome Developmental Center, but then things changed.

He was put into a van and driven to Syracuse Developmental Center (SDC) in Syracuse, NY. He had never been there before, and until he was in the van, he was unaware that he was being transferred permanently. He was given no chance to say goodbye to anyone, and he had not been told anything about the place that was supposed to be his new home. "I had really wanted to get out of Rome, and I didn't know if this institution was going to be any better than Rome or worse," he thought once he arrived.

He soon found out that SDC was better, despite the fact that it was still an institution. Like in Rome, Michael lived on a ward with twenty other people, but he no longer slept in a "big crib" or wore oversized jumpsuits. He had a real bed and he got to wear his own clothes. The rooms were cleaner than he was used to at RDC as well. More importantly, the staff seemed more caring and the residents had a lot more freedom. No longer was Michael shoved into a secluded ward whenever a stranger visited; in fact, all the residents could move freely throughout the facility. Even better, they could do so unsupervised. This small measure of freedom meant a great deal to Michael, since he could find friends with similar tastes and interests rather than simply doing his best to get along with the people in his unit. He soon found kindred spirits in the therapy department and developed close relationships with several staff members there.

Michael quickly discerned that the director of SDC, Dr. Michael Dillon, was sincerely interested in making life in SDC as normal and pleasant as possible for everyone who lived and worked there. Dr. Dillon had an open mind and an open door for residents like Michael who wanted to make changes. Michael describes him as "an all around genuine person as far as trying to make a difference, not only for me, but for other people as well...He went to bat for people." Dr. Dillon did his best to adhere to the myriad, often conflicting state and federal regulations designed to ensure the safety of all the residents and staff, while at the same time ensuring that SDC was as homelike as possible. As Michael says, "the residents had rights and he tried to enforce that they did have rights, but [...] trying to do what the state says [...] and trying to make it as personal for the people who lived there -- there were some things he couldn't do and some things he could do." One of the things Dr. Dillon did, and did well, was listen – and one of the things Michael did well, and had always longed to do at RDC, was talk about ways to make life in the institution more bearable. As they got to know each other, the two men developed a relationship of mutual respect. Michael presented his ideas for improvement and gained new insights into the administrative aspects of managing a residential facility while Dr. Dillon had the opportunity to see SDC through the eyes of one of its residents.

Michael remembers how he and Dr. Dillon wrangled about the doors at SDC. Although all were wide enough to permit wheelchairs and rolling beds to pass through easily, they did not open automatically. This meant that residents with limited strength or mobility could not leave their rooms or roam the facility without enlisting the aid of someone capable of opening the heavy doors, which had been designed with fire safety rather than ease of access in mind. While Michael understood the need for safety, he insisted that SDC could not claim to be a "least restrictive environment" unless it had automatic doors that any resident could open and close. His persistence won out in the end; even though SDC was slated to close down permanently and Dr. Dillon was supposed to focus on transitioning residents to other, smaller housing options, he eventually ordered the installation of automatic doors.

This small victory made a huge difference in Michael's life. For the first time, he had the sense that an administrator – a man of authority who had power over nearly every aspect of Michael's life – was actually interested in hearing what Michael had to say. Even though he was a ward of the state, a resident of an institution that used to be called an idiot asylum and a man with a severe disability, Michael could make his voice heard and ensure that important changes were made.

Not only was life in SDC better for Michael; he finally had the chance to have a life outside of the institution as well. Soon after he moved to SDC, Michael enrolled at a local public school, Corcoran High School. Initially, Michael was placed in a special class for students with disabilities. Instead of following the regular curriculum, the teacher devised individual education plans for Michael and his classmates so they could learn at their own pace. While an educational program tailored to his needs and abilities was a welcome change for Michael, he did not like being segregated from the non-disabled students. He had little chance to interact with typical teenagers because his classroom was at the back of the school building in a separate wing constructed solely for "handicapped" classes. Still, Michael remembers high school positively: "I had fun at Corcoran because it was another way I got out of the institution." Although it was very hard for Michael because he was so far behind the other students, he liked school and hoped he could someday earn a high school diploma.

At the same time, Michael registered for a continuing education course offered by a unique new program for adults with developmental disabilities. The original concept for this program, called 'College for Living', was modeled on a similar program at Metropolitan Community College in Denver, Colorado. Parents, community members, and staff at the Center on Human Policy had learned about this program and wanted to initiate something similar locally. At their suggestion, Dr. Dillon agreed to use some of SDC's recreation therapy funds to hire a coordinator. Onondaga Community College agreed to donate a small office and allow the College for Living to use its classrooms. Syracuse University faculty in the School of Education contributed by incorporating work with College for Living students into the requirements for their undergraduate courses. This arrangement benefitted everyone, as the students of education gained hands-on experience and the College for Living students got to spend quality time with their non-disabled peers as well as learning valuable new skills. Volunteers filled additional positions.

When Michael enrolled in the College for Living, most classes were either recreational (e.g. crafts, dance, music, bowling, horseback riding) or devoted to developing practical skills like writing job applications or managing money. The College also offered some personal skills courses that addressed topics rarely taught in traditional special education classes, like first aid, personal hygiene, dating and sexuality. About a third of the two hundred students lived in SDC, like Michael, but the remaining two-thirds lived with their families or in supported living situations in the area. The classes ran on the community college schedule so Michael had plenty of opportunities to mingle with the rest of the student body. The coordinator, Sue Lehr, not only recruited the volunteers, provided training and support, managed the budget and schedule and facilitated contact among the various administrators and professors, but also taught one class per term. She recalls how important teaching was, as it gave her "some credibility with my 'staff' [to] be able to understand their concerns." Michael signed up for her very first class, a recreational course focusing on arts and crafts.

During the initial class meeting, Sue invited the students to look through craft magazines for ideas and laid out a variety of materials for them to explore, including clay, beads, paints, charcoals, colored pencils and pastel chalks. She encouraged Michael and his nine classmates to think about making something of value and importance; something another adult might appreciate seeing or owning. She remembers Michael in particular because he said, "I want to make a wallet, a leather wallet. I want something to hold all the money I'm going to make." Sue was impressed with his drive and conviction when he made this announcement:

> I stared at him for a moment or two. Here was this skinny, almost fragile looking young man, perched in a wheelchair that clearly was too small for him and which had a hand-made wooden seat, painted bright red. He was wearing faded jeans, a NASCAR T-shirt, and a great pair of cowboy boots. His hair was black and bushy, like an Afro, but Michael was white. He had the most beguiling smile and a twinkle in his eye that made me question what he was saying. He laughed and when he did, his arms flew up in a jerky spastic motion and his one leg thumped up and down on the foot tread on his wheel chair. Was he kidding, serious, making fun of me, testing me? I had no idea.

Michael did make a leather wallet that spring, and the foundation for a lasting friendship was laid.

Michael soon emerged as a leader among the College for Living students - not only the students from Syracuse Developmental Center, but also the other students who came to know him in class or during lunch in the dining hall, where lively conversations often took place. He encouraged them to speak out about whatever moved them and listened carefully when they did. Sue Lehr says, "It didn't take long to realize that these students were engaging, trusting, informative and provocative. I am not sure what assumptions I had about adults with mental retardation and developmental disabilities, but I quickly learned that, just like everyone else, when given the chance they would tell you what they wanted, needed and deserved." Michael had always been quick to speak out, but now he realized more and more how much he could accomplish.

With time and more chances to make his voice heard not only among his peers, but also within the larger community, Michael gained maturity and self-confidence. He began to see new ways to work for change and became interested in working for the rights of people with disabilities in general. And he made real friends. He had buddies in his classes and pals to hang out with at SDC in the evenings. He remembers, "It got to the point where I became like an adopted brother to one of the staff there. Her roommate also worked at SDC." Michael often went to their house for dinner and they "just became good friends", talking and laughing together for hours.

Even with a widening circle of friends and much more freedom than he had ever known, though, SDC was not a home. The more he grew, the more certain he became that he did not want to be a resident of an institution anymore. He was tired of being handled and managed, tired of following schedules made for the group instead of the individual, tired of having so little privacy. It bothered him that he could not have visitors without staff supervision and that even the smallest changes required lengthy negotiations. His friends among the staff saw how frustrated he was and encouraged him to explore alternatives. They asked him repeatedly, "Michael, what are you doing here? You don't belong here." He agreed, and he soon went to the director to announce his goal of moving out. Dr. Dillon was supportive, as Michael recalls. "He knew that I wasn't afraid, and he helped me because he knew I [...] wanted out of SDC." Moving out was not a simple matter, though, since there were few housing options for people like Michael, who still needed substantial help to manage everyday tasks.

The chance came in 1982, when Michael attended a picnic at the home of a friend, Cheli Paetow. He had met Cheli when she worked at SDC in the late 1970s and they stayed in touch even after she moved on to another job. She was the one who first told him about the College for Living. When Cheli heard that the College for Living was hosting an open house, she offered to drive Michael there. She has a fond memory of "securing Mike, still in his wheelchair, into the back bed of my pick-up and driving him [to the open house...] Though certainly risky and unacceptable by current transportation safety standards, I used the same method to get Mike to a party at my house." Cheli had invited a bunch of friends and colleagues to this picnic, one of whom was Carole Hayes Collier. As soon as Carole saw Michael arrive in the back of the pick-up, she recognized that he was probably one of the Willowbrook class. They struck up a conversation and Carole told Michael about some new supported apartments in downtown Syracuse slated to open later that year. The United Cerebral Palsy Association was running them and looking for potential residents.[44] She asked whether Michael might be interested, and of course, he immediately said he was. Carole explained that the apartments were intended to help residents of institutions to get used to living in the community and develop independent living skills before they moved on to places of their own. Even better, the United Cerebral Palsy Association anticipated having the apartments ready for new residents in just a few months.

Michael started gathering information about this opportunity as soon as possible. He found out that the apartments were set up with wheelchair users in mind — not only were they fully accessible, but the kitchen and bath had been designed so that Michael would be able to use all the appliances with minimal or no assistance. The apartments were conveniently located downtown in an area

with lots of pedestrian traffic and curb cuts, so it would be possible
for Michael to get around on his own. Even better, the staff seemed
enthusiastic about helping Michael and his future housemates be as
independent as possible. There were some downsides, though, which
Michael considered carefully before agreeing to move in. For one
thing, he would have to share a bedroom, which was not the end
of the world, but also not ideal. More troubling was the fact that
the apartment program was funded by Medicaid as an "Intermediate
Care Facility - Mental Retardation" (abbreviated ICF-MR). This
meant that the regulations governing the apartments were similar to
those in the institution. Staff members were required to keep detailed
records about the residents, including how often they used the bathroom and when they took their medications, etc. The regulations
also required that various safety notices be posted throughout the
living space, which detracted from the homeliness of the apartments.
After substantial research and long talks with the administrators of
SDC and the United Cerebral Palsy Association, Michael decided to
seize this chance to escape SDC and get the help he knew he might
need to live independently.

On August 10, 1982, Michael left the institution behind him and
moved into his own place with three other men. He recalls, "coming
from an institution into this supportive housing, I loved it at the time.
I had a little bit more freedom and control." He and his housemates
soon became friends and they enjoyed going out together. It was
wonderful to be able to go to the movies, shopping or even just for
a walk downtown without dealing with bureaucracy. The staff was
friendly and motivated as well. Michael remembers how exciting it
was to finally take charge of his own banking. In the beginning, a
staff member went to the bank with Michael to make sure he did
not run into trouble, but after a while Michael could take care of
his financial matters himself. He learned to cook a bit and relished
the freedom to simply go to the fridge and root around whenever
he felt like having a snack. Even though it annoyed him that a sign
detailing the procedure for the use and cleaning of portable urinals
adorned the dining room wall, the relative independence he enjoyed

was worth it. It was a new beginning and Michael was determined to make the most of it.

7

"I don't let my disability stand in my way."[45]

The chance to move out of SDC marked a milestone in Michael's personal life, and he soon discovered that it brought important changes to his professional life as well. When he first moved in, he was still enrolled at Corcoran High School even though he was far older than the average high school student. He wanted to complete the requirements to earn a diploma, but the school administrators told him he would need at least an extra year to do so. Since he had received minimal education before moving to SDC, Michael lacked basic knowledge and study skills that his classmates had been developing over decades. He was finally allowed to leave the special education wing and attend regular classes as a "mainstreamed" student, but the school failed to provide any useful support, accommodations or adaptations to the curriculum that would have enabled Michael to succeed. From the school's perspective, simply placing Michael in regular classes was enough to guarantee him an education in the "least restrictive environment" even though Michael's physical limitations and educational history made it impossible for him to participate meaningfully without assistance.

Michael tried his best but the workload was overwhelming – "just like ramming a lot of stuff into one year." He knew he would not pass and so he decided to drop out. It just made no sense to continue going to school when he knew a diploma was out of his reach, and he realized that he was wasting time he could be using to grow in other directions. Still, the situation was infuriating, especially because he knew how much his parents had always hoped he would get an education. He remembers how disgusted he was with the entire situation: "At the end of it, I was asked to go to graduation to get my letter of attendance. I said, 'NO!' I decided I was not going to get something on a piece of paper just for the number of days I was in school. They sent it to me in the mail and I just threw it away."

Fortunately, Michael had already begun to explore alternatives. Having enrolled in the College for Living, he realized there were many ways to define an education and he knew that he had a lot to contribute even without a diploma. His initial attempts to find a meaningful job were not particularly encouraging, though. Soon after he quit school, Michael signed up for a vocational program, but it was canceled before it even started. Because no other appropriate program existed at the time, Michael attended an informal day program at the UCP center that focused on daily living skills and vocational counseling. He also went to a sheltered workshop for a weeklong evaluation. At the time, sheltered workshops were the employment option most commonly recommended for people with severe disabilities like Michael. Sheltered workshops employ only people with disabilities, usually to do simple, menial tasks like data entry, product assembly or mail preparation. The workers are paid a token wage below the legal minimum and the operational and personnel costs of running the workshop are usually subsidized by the state or a private organization. The original idea behind sheltered workshops was not unlike the motivation for Charles Bernstein's colonies at the Rome State School back in the 1920s; while there, people with disabilities would learn important vocational skills, produce useful goods and contribute to their communities without facing the stresses of the normal workplace. Ostensibly, workers who made 'progress' in such a segregated environment could eventually move on to 'real' jobs elsewhere, although such cases were rare. This was not what Michael envisioned for himself, but at age 22 with no other options, it seemed worth trying.

Michael's experience during his trial week was disheartening. He was given the task of typing addresses on envelopes, which was not only mind-numbingly dull for him, but also quite difficult since he could only type using one finger. He overheard people there talking about how slow he was, commenting that he probably should not be paid as much as faster workers. The prospect of spending his days in such an environment was not attractive, especially because he knew the job would never let him show, let alone build on, his actual abilities. He recalls wryly, "I know that my best strength is to use my voice and my speaking ability and my ability to think and organize things. Sitting in a room doing piecework is just not my cup of tea."

Luckily for Michael, Carole Hayes Collier had not forgotten about him. She knew he had moved out of SDC and remembered his engaging manner. When she heard from Diane Murphy that Dr. Robert Bogdan, a professor at Syracuse University, was interested in inviting a former inmate of an institution talk to his students, Michael immediately sprang to mind. With Diane's help, Michael began visiting Dr. Bogdan's classes and telling about his life and experiences. He was in his element – and Diane and Carole were not the only ones who noticed a "transformation" in him. Diane remembers thinking that "Michael was the model for change. He was leading the change."

Steven Taylor, another professor at Syracuse University and the Director of the Center on Human Policy, recognized Michael's talents and sought to recruit him for a new initiative – a self-advocacy project. The idea behind self-advocacy was simple: people with disabilities knew best what their needs and wishes were, so they should take the lead in determining the kinds of services and supports they needed and the directions their lives should take. This idea was related to another emerging concept called self-determination, which emphasized disabled people's right to participate in decisions affecting them. Self-determination was a term most often employed by non-disabled professionals in the disability studies field and focused on the idea of giving more choices to people with disabilities. The key difference was that self-advocacy was essentially powered by people with disabilities themselves. Michael explains, "we should have real choices, not just the choices that other people give us." At the Center on Human Policy, people like Steve Taylor realized that people with disabilities needed to build their own networks and learn how to advocate for themselves, and for that, they needed a leader who was not only a good listener and organizer, but also someone who was not afraid to speak out. Michael was the perfect man for the job.

The Self-Advocacy project that Michael was hired to work on at the Center on Human Policy was funded by a grant from the Stuart Mott Foundation and involved identifying and helping people with disabilities in different locations to coalesce and form constituent groups. The primary goal of these groups would be to affect and implement new changes within the human service systems, within their respective communities, by confronting existing policies of institutionalization, isolation, abandonment, and total devaluation of human beings who happened to have disabilities. Of course, this was a daunting task, but Michael and his colleague Pat Killius attacked it with gusto. Another member of the Willowbrook class, Pat had also spent years living in institutions and was no stranger to the kind of abuse and neglect that was common in such facilities. She was a strong supporter of self-advocacy because she had learned the hard way, "if I don't talk about my own needs, then they will never be met."[46]

Michael and Pat's job involved meeting with other potential self-advocates around New York State to identify and clarify the issues they believed were most pressing. Michael and Pat arranged for helpers to record their statements and transcribe them later. Back at the Center on Human Policy, the two of them rehashed the key ideas that had emerged during their meetings and brainstormed about ways to convey the kinds of changes that were necessary. Then, in collaboration with colleagues, Michael and Pat developed a presentation that addressed those issues directly in a way that would inspire change and promote immediate action. Their presentations always began by inviting discussions about the importance of self-advocacy and speaking out before moving on to the specific goals they wanted to achieve. Sometimes they developed informational brochures as well. For them, the key was to "show others how to fight for their rights and use the responsibilities that go with them."[47] Michael had found his calling. "I believe in self-advocacy because I feel that disabled people have the right to do anything that non-disabled people can do," he wrote later. "I feel that people with developmental disabilities or mental retardation should not be segregated from non-disabled and that we should be able to get the proper training for jobs and get the proper education."[48]

At first, Michael and Pat focused on creating local networks and recruiting other self-advocates, but as they gained confidence and experience, they expanded the scope of their activities. They worked together with other people at the Center on Human Policy to disseminate information, encourage people to speak out and promote change within the state systems that administered programs for people with disabilities. They also began to recruit other self-advocates to make presentations to their local organizations. In their efforts, they encountered a new organization with similar values and goals: TASH.[49] TASH was founded by a group of parents and "audacious researchers" who realized that "no other organization was addressing the ideological, research, financial and programmatic rights and needs of people with severe disabilities; the most vulnerable, segregated, abused, neglected and denied people in our society."[50] They saw disability rights in the context of the larger civil rights movement and wanted to open a forum for parents, academics and most importantly, people with disabilities themselves, to challenge the system – a system that served to segregate, isolate and control people with disabilities because it was defined and perpetuated by "continuum tolerators" and "ruling professionals".[51] Self-advocacy was a crucial component of TASH's vision.

Michael and Pat recognized the vast potential of TASH for the self-advocacy movement. It was both invigorating and a little scary to work with so many people who were passionate about disability rights, who listened intently but also spoke out – and did not always agree. Although everyone was committed to defending the civil rights of people with disabilities, the organization had to deal with "numerous stresses and strains having largely to do with the desire on the part of self-advocates to have TASH be their organization as its primary mission, versus the researchers, trainers and other, primarily university based, persons who wanted to keep TASH as a scientifically oriented forum for credible public policy."[52] Although every self-advocacy group sought to train and support self-advocates to present their issues with dignity and clarity, those issues varied from state to state and from group to group. In some areas, self-advocates' main goal was to close institutions, which meant convincing policymakers to replace them with community-based services to address the various needs of people with different disabilities. In states where deinstitutionalization was already underway, some self-advocates focused on lobbying elected officials and pushing for legislation to improve access to education, community programs and services and meaningful employment. Others sought to expand the role and presence of people with disabilities in their communities, highlighting the need for more inclusive social opportunities where real friendships and relationships could develop. The diversity of motives and goals within the self-advocacy movement was astounding and at times challenging, but also empowering for Michael and his friends and colleagues.

At the same time, Michael and many other self-advocates realized how important it was to explain their ideas and goals to people without disabilities, especially those who wanted to help. Self-advocates needed many kinds of help, but they did not need the patronizing attitude that often accompanied it. Even well-meaning helpers often insulted people with disabilities, albeit unknowingly. Michael's experiences in public rest rooms exemplify this issue. Because of the severity of his cerebral palsy, he has always needed assistance in the rest room, and it is not always possible to arrange for a male personal care attendant. On the few occasions when Michael had to use a public bathroom with a female helper, people's reactions were telling. In the men's room, Michael had to deal with suggestive or even lewd comments about his relationship with his attendant, while women in the ladies' room were more likely to react with pity, even falling over themselves to help Michael in any way they thought he might need. Neither reaction was comfortable for Michael; while the sexual innuendos made by fellow men were insulting, it was sometimes more degrading to be treated like a child by well-meaning women in the ladies' room. For this reason, Michael and Pat Killius made it one of their priorities to develop informational materials for non-disabled support people, telling them how their actions might be perceived by the people they sought to assist. The headline of one of the brochures they helped to develop says it all: "Wanted: trustworthy, wise guide - not bossy".[53]

Another challenge was the need to address the very real concerns and even fears of parents of people with disabilities who were overwhelmed by the logistical challenges of helping their children live independent, self-determined lives. Parents were used to being advocates for their children and naturally did not always find it easy to let their children take over that role. This was especially true of parents whose children could not voice their desires clearly. Michael recalls a trip to Oklahoma with a few colleagues from the Center on Human Policy to talk to members of the growing self-advocacy network there. Their goal was to support and assist families and residents with their intention to close Hissom Memorial Center, an institution with close to six hundred inmates with disabilities. Not surprisingly, the team encountered opposition on a bureaucratic level, but when they met with parents and families of individuals housed at Hissom, Michael realized that some of them were reluctant as well. The idea of having their children move out of Hissom was frightening for many, even though they knew conditions there deserved improvement. Michael acknowledged their fears but also warned them that, from his experiences, how their children were being treated behind the walls of the locked wards and "day rooms," was far more frightening. He spoke with passion about his personal experiences at Rome and Syracuse Developmental Centers. He knew what his life should have been, and he knew what the reality was for people like him who lived behind institutional walls. He reminded them that they, the families and the people with disabilities, could be the agents of change.

Michael's personal stories and call to action complemented the wealth of information and strategies the team brought with them, ranging from sample policy statements to guidelines for identifying key potential allies in the general community, state government and political parties. The results were gratifying; after a class-action suit alleging that residents of Hissom were "subject to abuse, neglect, injury, and unnecessary physical and chemical restraints and were denied adequate medical care, clothing, food, and habilitation services", the district court judge ruled in favor of deinstitutionalization and "community-based alternative placements".[54]

Through the Center on Human Policy and the network of self-advocates, academics, parents and professionals he developed while working there, Michael could finally make his voice heard in a way that brought real improvements to the lives of people with disabilities across the country. He knew he was doing important work that he was uniquely equipped to do, in a job that utilized his strengths and abilities. As he won the respect of others, he gained confidence and began to envision his own future in new ways.

8

Moving on

As Michael's professional career took off and he met more and more interesting people, he became increasingly disillusioned with the supported apartment where he lived. He had known that it had downsides when he moved in, but these seemed insignificant in comparison with the treatment he had experienced in Rome and SDC. After a few years, though, he realized he was not only ready to move on; he was desperate to do so. He "needed to live someplace without all the goals, verbal prompts, and the control" that a Medicaid-funded apartment entailed. Just like in the institution, he had no power to hire or fire the staff responsible for assisting him, and the rate of turnover was high. It seemed like he was forever training new personal care attendants, and he was tired of hearing staff bicker and complain. The apartment felt less and less like a home, but alternatives were hard to find. One day Michael reached the end of his rope. The staff were too busy fighting with one another to notice his distress. Although he rarely drank more than the occasional beer, he fled the apartment and got drunk at a local bar. When he finally returned, he broke down; he knew he needed to get out, but he did not know how. The next day he went to the supervisor in charge of the apartment and told her that he wanted to leave. He had acquired all the daily living skills this "transitional" living situation was supposed to teach him and he knew he could grow no further in this environment. The supervisor was sympathetic but, like Michael, knew of no better options. Together with his family, Michael decided to apply for a place in a Small Residential Unit (SRU) in Tupper Lake. The plan was for him to live there for a short time while his parents made the necessary arrangements to allow him to move back in with them. His parents were eager to have him close by and believed they could manage having him live in their home. The SRU was hardly different from his current apartment, but it seemed like a viable temporary solution. The one huge downside was that it was too far from Syracuse for Michael to keep his job at the Center on Human Policy, and there was no chance he would find an equally rewarding position in rural Tupper Lake. He loved his work, but when he really thought about it, he was willing to sacrifice it for the chance to live in a real home.

Michael enlisted the aid of one of the personal attendants, a man named Paul, to fill out the necessary application forms for the SRU. Paul had been working at the apartment for about two years and Michael knew him as one of the few who "went the extra steps to make people feel like it was their home instead of a program or an institution." Paul helped, dutifully filling in all the required information, even though he believed the move was not in Michael's best interest. In fact, nearly everyone who knew Michael tried to talk him out of it, but Paul was the only one who came up with a viable alternative. He did not want Michael to have to give up his job and everything he had accomplished in his professional life, but he understood that Michael felt backed into a corner. Paul liked Michael and he had heard about a new program called "consumer-directed care" that paid for live-in help for people with disabilities. He and his housemate, Oscar, both found the idea of living with Michael appealing and they were willing to provide the help that Michael needed. After they had talked it over, Paul called Michael and asked him if he would consider moving in with him and Oscar. Michael remembers being "tickled" by the offer, but also wary of getting into another situation where he felt managed and controlled rather than valued. He wanted Paul as a friend and housemate, not an official caregiver responsible for making reports about him and his habits. Paul agreed, so he and Michael went to the director of the funding agency and laid out their conditions. Michael made clear what he wanted:

> First: that I don't have any goals written on paper and that this place would really be my home. Second: I didn't want anything posted all over the walls, especially stuff that was my personal business. And I wanted control over my life to pay my own bills, to come and go as I pleased, and to be able to leave this program when I felt that it was time to move on. I wanted to go to something better.

Fortunately, this program was set up to support the kind of home life that Paul and Michael envisioned. The director assured them that the required paperwork was minimal, hardly more than was required for any other job, and there would be no intrusive assessment. In fact, the program required the county office in charge of long term care to evaluate what kinds of help Michael needed and how many hours of service it would take to provide this help – but together with Michael. Michael would assume responsibility for hiring, training and supervising his own assistants and the agency would simply support him when he needed it, either by helping to train people or consulting over the phone. Michael could allot the hours his staff worked in any way that made sense for him and his assistants, so there were no pre-determined schedules that had to be followed. The director would visit once a month to see how things were going, but that was all. It sounded like the ideal solution – if they could find a house to live in. This promised to be a daunting task.

In fact, finding an accessible house for three proved to be much easier than anyone expected, in part because Michael had such a strong network of friends and acquaintances. Michael remembers the fortuitous turn of events. "This woman who worked at ENABLE and I were talking one day. I was telling her about my move and I joked with her, saying, "Why don't you buy a house that could be made accessible so that I can rent it from you?" She was in real estate on a part time basis, but I was just kidding. And then she had told me that she had already done it! She took Paul and I over to see the house later that same day."

On September 30, 1988, Michael, Paul and Oscar moved into their new house. Things got off to a rocky start because the regulations stipulated that state funds could not be used to build a wheelchair ramp for the front door until a wheelchair user was a resident of the house, which meant that Michael had to move in before he could actually get in the door. Other funding agencies, unused to this novel living situation, put up bureaucratic hurdles that created financial difficulties as well. Eventually, though, Paul and Michael managed to work everything out. Paul became Michael's full-time personal care assistant, but in the context of the new consumer-directed care program that meant Michael was officially his supervisor. It was important to both of them that Paul be a roommate, not an employee, so Michael hired some staff to help him with his morning and evening routines and do his share of the housekeeping. Still, he knew he could always rely on Paul for help if he needed it, so he did not have to worry if a staff member was late or sick. He and Paul even pooled their money to buy a wheelchair van so they could go out together whenever they felt like it.

Michael and Paul were really happy with their new living situation. Michael loved that he knew from day to day who was going to be there and at what time, and that he had the final word over his daily routine. In Rome and SDC, schedules were made according to staff needs, so if that meant serving dinner at 4:30 in the afternoon and sending everyone to bed at seven, residents had to put up with it. In the supported apartment where Michael had lived before, he had more control over the daily schedule but he often had no idea who would arrive to help him out of bed in the morning or who would be there in the evening; he had to work with whomever the agency sent, whether he knew the person or not. Since staff turnover was high and the agency managed a number of apartments, many assistants did not have the opportunity to develop good working relationships with the people they served, and their commitment to the job was not always as strong as Michael could have wished. This meant that when the agency was short of staff, some jobs simply did not get done. Michael recalls, "If they can't find anyone to fill your hours for that day, you may not be able to get out of bed, for example." Once he was in charge of his own assistants, though, he never had to worry about problems like this; if someone were ill or snowed in (which is not unusual in Central New York's harsh winters) they could just call Michael and let him know, rather than calling an agency representative who might or might not be able to organize a replacement. Michael was very pleased with this arrangement. He felt that his aides had a real commitment to him. They had the time and incentive to learn his ways and therefore did not need constant direction, and because Michael was their supervisor, they could negotiate their hours and work schedules with him directly. This made for a comfortable professional relationship. As Michael says, "We know each other well."

In September of 1990, Paul, Oscar, and Michael decided to move to Georgia. Michael and Paul had visited Atlanta to attend a conference, and Paul had reconnected with a branch of his family who lived there. When the possibility of a job down south emerged, Michael decided he was also ready for a change. The three men moved down together. With this move, Paul was no longer receiving any reimbursement for living with Michael, but they were all confident that they could make it work. At this point Michael felt comfortable in the role of staff supervisor and Paul was, as always, willing to pick up any slack if Michael needed time to get his schedule organized. Unfortunately, the jobs they had arranged did not pan out as they had planned and after a year, they decided to move back to Central New York. Michael spent a few months living in Tupper Lake with his parents, and then he and Paul became housemates again in Syracuse. Michael was able to resume his position at the Center on Human Policy and he and Paul settled back in to their old routine.

It was an exciting time to be at the Center on Human Policy. Before he moved to Georgia, Michael had been instrumental in setting up a statewide network of self-advocates. He and Pat Killius had long wanted to establish an official agency that would coordinate activities of self-advocates and their supporters statewide and maintain links to national organizations like TASH. Their hard work paid off in March 1990, when Michael helped to found the Self-Advocacy Association of New York State. Its seat was in Schenectady and its regional chapters were responsible for working with local groups. Michael had hoped to pursue similar aims in Georgia, but when that proved impossible, he was happy to return to the Center on Human Policy and pick up where he left off. As part of his regional chapter of the new Association, which was responsible for activities in thirteen New York counties, Michael's main job was to give presentations about self-advocacy to "pretty much anyone who wants to know."

Michael soon discovered how much he liked doing transition planning with high school students, since one of his major goals had always been to help young people learn to advocate for themselves. After working with both high schoolers and their parents, Michael realized that the transition from school to the workplace was even harder for many families because they had trouble negotiating how and when youth with disabilities should begin taking responsibility for their own life choices. In many ways, this problem results from the progress that has been made in Michael's lifetime. "A lot of the younger kids don't have a clue about self-advocacy [...] and I think the parents are scared of it too. They want their child to live at home with them forever, and the thought of them having their own place just doesn't work for them. You see, they forget where we have been. They didn't have to make the choices our parents made, to put us away in institutions and all. They have always had lots of support and services." Michael learned to advocate for himself because no one else could do it for him, but today's youth often have much more extensive support networks and they can easily forget how important it is for them to assert their right to make decisions about their lives.

Michael took on another exciting project as well: he and some colleagues convinced the State of New York to fund a pilot project to devise new, innovative ways of supporting people with disabilities individually. Although many more supports and services are available now than Michael ever had growing up, most are geared toward meeting a general need rather than serving individuals personally. From his own experience in the supported apartment, Michael knew how crucial it was to develop a system that made professionals and service providers think in terms of support packages tailored to each person. This is how he describes the problem: "A lot of people feel they can just put disabled people in a home together, as though because we are disabled we'll have the same interests. They feel we'll put up with it. Well, we shouldn't have to put up with it. It's like, how do you know what's best for me when [...] you don't even treat me as an individual or a person, you just assume that you come in, do your eight hours and then, that's it. Rather than helping us deal with our problems, all you care about is drugging us up and that will be the end of that." Michael knew from experience that one of the biggest barriers to more individually organized services was coordination; people with disabilities needed a means to explore the available options and identify potentially useful programs, determine their eligibility and organize the logistics and funding. Most needed support to undertake this daunting task, but they did not want professionals taking over their decisions and their lives in the process.

At the Center, Michael and his colleagues developed a model based on a novel idea: since every service exists for the sake of the individual, the individual should hold decision-making power and delegate it as he or she saw fit, assisted and supported by trustworthy allies. The model proposed that each person in need of services would invite such allies to join a circle of support, whose members would help the person make decisions about his or her life and serve as the first level of support. Together with the circle, the person would then identify a service coordinator to help implement those decisions. On the next level up, service brokers familiar with the range of options available would help service coordinators identify the programs or services best suited to the person's needs and desires and facilitate the creation of a useful package. The system's guiding principle was the conviction that decisions should always be made at the lowest level possible to ensure that the individual remained the central focus. The beauty of the system, Michael says, is that "it really depends on what a person needs as to how big their circles are, or how complicated their services are."

Michael is proud of the work he did on this program because he has seen the meaningful difference it has made in people's lives. One of Michael's friends, who became disabled after an accident, is a perfect example. Once he was released from the hospital, this friend moved back in with his mother, but because he needed special equipment to breathe, he never left his room. His mother managed his life, arranging for the services she thought he needed and using the money he received for his care as she saw fit. Finally, one of his friends, who happened to be a nurse, said that he had to get out of that room or he would die in it. Michael recalls, "that was my friend's worst fear: that he would die there, all alone."

Fortunately, the nurse had heard about the project Michael had been working on. She helped their mutual friend set up a circle of support and agreed to be his service coordinator so he could live on his own in an apartment, with the services and supports he needed coming in to his own place. Now he decides who is going to work with him and what kinds of help he needs. Though his care costs over $65,000 a year, it would cost many times that to keep him in a nursing home — and now he has control over his life. Even more important, Michael's friend has found a purpose in life that would never have been possible in his old room at his mother's house. He has become a painter, using his mouth to hold the brush. Every day he works with four different kindergarten classes and loves his job as much as the kids seem to love him. Michael says the difference in his life is reflected in his art: "When he painted at home his pictures were really dark and gloomy [but] his paintings use brighter colors now."

Michael's most recent project involves developing a curriculum for Disability Awareness Week for schools. He would like it to be mandatory for all the schools in New York State to host a Disability Awareness Week, but the legislature still has to approve the plan. Michael envisions organizing self-advocates to go into schools and teach people – students, staff and administrators – about disability issues in general and self-advocacy in particular. He hopes that raising awareness about the problems and challenges people with disabilities face will empower both self-advocates and their supporters. At the same time, Michael thinks it is crucial to ensure that people remember the conditions people with disabilities used to have to endure. "Well, I just keep thinking that people forget history. They forget that I took the risk to get out of [institutions] and because they never had to fight for nothing, they just think it is always going to be there for them. But I don't think so. We can't let anyone forget where we were. [...] There is a whole generation of kids who just have never had my experience. We can't let them forget."

9

The love of his life

Michael's colleagues at the Center on Human Policy missed him while he was in Georgia. He had become a valued member of the team and they told newcomers all about him. One of the new people was Lori Gardiner, who was doing an internship at the Center as part of her Master's degree in rehabilitation counseling. She says, "I had always heard about Michael Kennedy. He was on a leave of absence then, and people would tell me that I would be interested in meeting this Michael Kennedy. He was in Georgia at the time and then he relocated back here." Lori also has cerebral palsy, but her childhood and upbringing were very different from Michael's. She lived with her adoptive mother and sister at home, and she was expected and encouraged to be as independent as possible. She attended regular neighborhood schools and learned how to take care of herself with little or no assistance. Unlike Michael's parents, Lori's mother had access to community-based support services and made sure Lori received all the therapy she needed. She did not work full time, so she also had the time and energy to devote to teaching Lori and her sister, who also has a disability, all the skills they would need to function on their own. Lori recalls, "we were her whole life. She put all her heart into us to make us as independent as possible." Many of Michael's friends at the Center on Human Policy believed that Michael and Lori would hit it off, but Lori finished her internship at the Center before Michael returned and their paths never crossed.

Fortunately for Lori and Michael, a mutual friend made the effort to get them together. Lori was doing an internship at ENABLE that involved working with some of the people in the apartment where Michael used to live. One day when Michael was visiting old friends there, Lori happened to come by and their mutual friend jumped at the chance to introduce them to one another. Afterward, the friend told Michael all about Lori and convinced him to try asking her out on a date. Michael doubted his chances. "Here she was, all prim and proper, getting her education at Syracuse University." Would such a classy lady be interested in dating a guy who had not even finished high school? Lori was also shy at first; she knew her mother believed she was not ready for a relationship and she was very busy with her graduate program. She finally agreed to a date, though, and one soon turned into two, and three, and more.

Once the initial excitement of a new relationship shifted toward a deeper commitment, Michael and Lori realized marriage was the path they wanted to take. They took their time, though, spending more than two years getting to know one another and talking about their future together. Making a solemn, public commitment to each other meant the world to both of them and they eagerly planned their wedding with their families. Some of their family members were concerned about their plans and warned them not to idealize marriage. All of Michael's siblings had divorced and remarried more than once and his parents had certainly struggled throughout their lives together. His relatives were skeptical that a long-term commitment could work, especially given Michael's need for supported living and attendant care. However, Lori and Michael were confident that they knew what lay ahead and their love would help them to overcome any obstacles. In 1993, they exchanged vows and moved into a new apartment together. A new life was beginning for both of them.

Despite careful planning and honest, open discussions about every eventuality they could imagine, Lori and Michael's first few years as a married couple turned out to be rockier than they had hoped. Although they knew they wanted to be together, they soon realized that the vast differences between their previous life experiences presented more challenges than they had expected. Because Michael was never provided with appropriate therapies or education as a child, he missed the chance to develop the muscle control and skills that might have enabled him to live more independently. As a result, he was dependent on personal care assistants to help him with every aspect of daily life, from getting up and dressed in the morning to bathing and getting ready for bed at night – and everything in between. Lori knew this, but assumed that she would be able to take over a lot of the work. It was impossible for her to do as much as Paul had, though; with a full-time job, she had neither the time nor the energy to give Michael all the assistance he needed. Also, as her husband gently pointed out, "that's nice, but you have to remember that you have a disability yourself."

Lori was also used to a lot more privacy than Michael had ever known. Michael says of their first year of marriage, "she was not really grooving on the fact that we had aides coming in and out of our house all the time," but he understood how hard it was for her to accept the nearly constant presence of other people. Even worse, these people were neither family nor necessarily friends; they were employees who did all the things that employees in most businesses do. Sometimes they were early or late; sometimes they were efficient and sometimes clumsy; sometimes they were honest and sometimes they were not. Lori was horrified when one of the personal care attendants was caught stealing. Michael, an experienced staff supervisor by this point, understood Lori's discomfort but also knew that they were in a much better position than couples in supervised apartments who had to deal with a myriad of regulations and a mountain of paperwork on top of the normal workload. He tried to help Lori feel comfortable but sometimes she simply needed to escape.

The situation was complicated by the fact that Lori was reluctant to accept any personal care assistance for herself since she was perfectly capable of managing on her own. Her mother had always told her, 'You don't need help.' Because Lori was not one of their clients, attendants assigned to Michael were not supposed to provide support for her even though they lived together. This was not a problem when it came to helping Michael with bathing or dressing, but it made other parts of daily life more challenging than necessary – especially mealtimes. With a full-time job, Lori could not always manage to cook meals for both of them, but Michael's aides were only allowed to cook for him. Michael found it ridiculous that he was supposed to eat in front of his wife without sharing his meal with her, but Lori resisted applying for services that would allow the attendants to prepare food for both of them. For her whole life, she says, "I put my all into overcoming my disabilities as much as possible." It seemed like giving in to accept help she did not need.

Although both of their families wished them well, neither was able to offer the young couple a great deal of support during their first years together. Lori's mother had developed Alzheimer's disease while Lori was in college and no longer even recognized her daughter by the time she got married. Lori's sister always had an open door for her, but most of her other relatives had moved to Florida. Michael's brothers and sister had their own families and their own cares, and his parents were getting older. They never came to visit Syracuse and Lori often felt uncomfortable in the Kennedy home in Tupper Lake. Until Michael started working on this book and discussing his early life with his siblings, Lori believed that his family did not care about Michael as much as they should have. She did not understand why they had put Michael in a horrible institution and never taught him to be independent like she was. Lori also felt that Michael's family did not particularly like her. Only his father seemed to approve of her and her relationship with Michael, but he was very reserved. In fact, Michael's parents and siblings were not quite sure how to act around Lori, with her master's degree and independent spirit. They never showed her how proud they were of Michael's achievements and how glad they were that he had found the love of his life. Only much later, when they began to work on this book together, did Michael's family open up and help Lori realize how deeply they care. Lori says now, "It is amazing how, since Michael has been working on the book, his family has really come together. It's great." At the same time, she realizes now "how much they had to go through" and she can understand their decisions much better.

About a year into their marriage, Michael and Lori bought a home together. They hoped that having more space would solve some of the problems they experienced in their apartment. Soon, though, it became clear to both of them that Lori was really struggling. She resented how little time she had alone with Michael and loathed the attendants who seemed to invade every corner of their lives. To her, it seemed like she faced a choice between keeping her independence and having more time with Michael, since the only way to share quality time was to allow the attendants to take care of meals and housework for both of them. Unable to handle the pressures she felt, Lori decided to stay with her sister for a while so she would have the time and space to sort out her feelings.

This decision made Michael feel like he had to solve all the problems alone, which was not easy. He had done his best to make sure Lori knew what she was getting into before they married, so it was hard to bear her frustration with the facts of his life. He did not want to give up on Lori, though, so he thought hard about what was troubling her and asked friends and coworkers for help. Michael realized that Lori equated assistance with dependence, so he tried to show her that asking for help sometimes, when she needed it or when it just made life more convenient, was not the same as admitting helplessness. He sought out staff he thought she would like and feel comfortable with in their home because he figured out that part of her problem with his attendants was lack of trust. Finally, he began to understand that Lori was so unhappy in part because she felt guilty that she could not take care of him as well as she could take care of herself. She knew that he was not capable of her degree of independence, but she had convinced herself that she could take over a lot more of Michael's care than was actually feasible. It was hard for a successful professional like herself to admit that it was too much for her.

After many heart-to-heart conversations, Lori and Michael decided they were committed to making their marriage work regardless of how much effort it cost them. They were honest with one another about their fears and hopes and slowly built up the kind of trust that underpins a solid marriage. In this, their faith proved to be a source of increasing strength. Lori had always been a devout Christian and religion was an important part of her life and identity. Michael was raised a Catholic but had never developed a strong bond to his church. He valued Lori's trust in God but did not want to have religion forced on him. Lori saw that he needed to find faith in his own way and invited him to accompany her to church without pressing him. She simply told him of the courage she drew from her own faith and encouraged him to ask God for support and guidance. When their marriage seemed to be failing, Michael turned to God for help and realized that building up his own faith not only made him stronger, it made Lori stronger as well. Now Michael says, "I really rely on God's strength to help us with our relationship."

By their third anniversary, Lori and Michael had worked out their biggest problems and settled into a routine that worked for both of them. They both had good jobs and a nice place to live and they took every opportunity to travel together. One memorable trip was when they went to visit Michael's old roommate Paul, who had moved back to Georgia, for Thanksgiving. He and Michael had remained close friends despite the distance, and they took turns calling each other once or twice a month. When he invited them to come, Paul promised to provide all the assistance they needed since he wanted them to just enjoy themselves. He was a great host and took care of their every need, from helping Michael out of bed in the morning to cooking all the meals. "It was a great time, and it confirmed for me that our friendship was a lasting one," Michael affirms.[55] Sadly, Paul died not long ago. Michael will always remember him as a true friend who valued him for himself and helped him find a place where he could thrive.

With Lori's support, Michael was finally able to complete his education as well. Lori realized how much it bothered Michael that he had never completed high school, even though he had certainly made a success of himself without a diploma. She knew he was smart enough to do it if he could find a school willing to make the necessary accommodations. Lori encouraged Michael to see how

BOCES, the Board of Cooperative Educational Services might help. He was skeptical at first but finally began the process of applying to a program that would award him a General Equivalency Diploma, the equivalent of a high school degree. From the start, Michael was honest with the program administrators about his abilities and clear about his goals. He said, 'Look, I've got this disability and this is what I do for a living – advocate for people with disabilities like me – and this is what I need to do." The teachers and administrators helped Michael to devise a reasonable educational plan that would enable him to take the classes he needed without making sacrifices at work. It took Michael three years, but he earned his GED in the end. He was very proud of this accomplishment because he knew he had earned it honestly, not simply because he had shown up each day. His success was even sweeter when he found out his classmates had chosen him to be their graduation speaker. His mother's dream for him, formed so many years ago, had finally come true – because Michael never gave up on that dream and Lori gave him the courage to make it work.

Michael and Lori still face challenges, even though they have been able to realize many of their goals. Like most couples, they worry about their financial future. In addition to keeping up with mortgage and car payments and saving for retirement, Lori and Michael have to wrangle with Medicaid, the federal insurance program that pays for Michael's personal assistants and other health care needs, including his expensive electric wheelchair. A few years ago, Michael received notification that his Medicaid funding was being discontinued because his and Lori's salaries had increased to the point that they were no longer eligible for federal aid. Michael and Lori needed Medicaid funding to cover their health care and the costs of Michael's personal assistants even though they both had good jobs; they could only hire a fraction of the help Michael needed if they had to pay for everything themselves. When they asked how the situation could be resolved, Medicaid officials informed them that Michael would be eligible for financial support if he moved into a nursing home. Alternatively, they could divorce, eliminating Lori's income from the equation. Michael says, "Even before we were married, we knew we might face problems like this, and we chose to go ahead and were willing to fight the system. We could have just lived together and gotten benefits, but that would have violated our religious beliefs. We didn't think it was fair that the government can force people to make decisions that go against what they believe. Why shouldn't we be able to be married like other people, just because we have disabilities? So we decided to face it."

Michael's skill as a self-advocate and Lori's professionalism served them well in the nearly two-year struggle that ensued. They were not about to give up on the marriage and home they had worked so hard for just to satisfy some bureaucrats. After months of arguing back and forth with various Medicaid officials, Michael and Lori found a solution – not an ideal solution, but a compromise they could live with. Lori had to sign a statement of "spousal refusal" abdicating all financial responsibility for Michael's care. Michael had to reduce the number of hours he worked to keep his income low enough to qualify for Medicaid. He also had to agree to divert a substantial portion of his income to Medicaid. Michael recalls how unsatisfying this solution was: "I hated to do that because I feel responsible for the bills and I think I should be paying my fair share for things (other than my services) like food, house payment, clothing, van maintenance, etc." Lori hated the idea of officially refusing to support the man she had pledged before God to have and to hold, in sickness and in health. It was hard to accept that they would not be able to save as much for retirement as they hoped and that they would have to cut back on 'luxuries' like vacations. Yet both realized that this sacrifice had to be made if they wanted to continue living together as husband and wife in their own home. It sounds like a simple thing, but for people with disabilities, nothing is simple.

Now, having recently celebrated their twentieth wedding anniversary, Michael and Lori are looking forward to retirement when they will be able to relax and do more travelling. Since they never had children, they do not have to worry about college costs, so they hope to use their savings to visit relatives and friends more often. They are also thinking about moving to a warmer climate. On a trip to North Carolina, they were impressed with the kinds of services available for people with disabilities there. Plus, the thought of avoiding the snow and ice that plagues Syracuse in winter was very attractive. They still have more than a decade to go until they can stop working, and every day still brings new challenges. For the moment, though, they are happy with their home and their jobs, their circle of friends and their faith, and their ability to spend time together and with family.

Reflecting on his life, Michael says, "I want my legacy to be two things:

1. I want to tell my story of courage; and,

2. I want to teach the upcoming kids that there is a history to all of this, and they need to know it and not forget it.

I want my story to be a teaching tool for caregivers and I want parents to know that they can have something better for their child.

I know that my life will continue to change, but I feel good about that because I won't have to do it by myself. I really hope that other people with disabilities will get to experience the opportunities that I have experienced. There are so many people who haven't had the chance to learn about life because they've been sheltered and controlled. I know that there are many caring people out there who might be willing to help people with disabilities if they understood how to do it, and who would learn from us as well. Then, truly, nothing would stop us.

Appendix:

The Making Of...

"Just as secrets have a way of breaking loose, memories often have a way of breaking down. They elude us, aren't quite sharp enough, or fool us into remembering things that didn't quite happen that way. Yet much as a family inhabits a house, memories inhabit our stories, make them breathe, give them life. So we learn to live with the reality that what we remember is an imperfect version of what we know to be true."[56]

Michael's story was a long time in the making. Over the years, several friends sought to assist Michael with his autobiography, but none of the efforts resulted in the book Michael wanted. This project unfolded over a period of several years, with intensive interviews, painstaking research, and multiple visits to key people in Michael's life. Through it all, Michael's perseverance, energy and infectious humor kept everyone going.

Timing is everything with most things in life. Until a few years ago, Michael's mother was not ready to tackle the emotional story of Michael's childhood and institutionalization. She needed decades to gather the courage to speak about her inner anguish and set the record straight. It took time to let the story percolate inside her and soul-searching to find the right time to tell it. Michael waited for years for his mother to reach this point, and at first, he was not even sure that she was ready. When we started talking about this project, he did not know if his mother would agree to be interviewed. When she did, he was concerned that she might not want her real name used. He hoped his siblings would agree to share their stories and allow Michael to use his mother's stories about them, but he was not certain they would agree. To his surprise, everyone wanted to help him, and their stories revealed their appreciation of Michael's fighting spirit and their pride in his accomplishments. As with most memoirs, it is hard to know where you will end up when you are on such a journey.

As qualitative researchers, Janet and Sue were concerned about getting Michael's story pieced together in a way that presented the facts but highlighted what the main characters endured at the time. We interviewed Michael over a two-year period, meeting in various places, including the community room at his condominium complex, his place of work, and in the community. Each interview, which we recorded, lasted approximately one hour. We used an open-ended interviewing style, allowing the conversation to follow a particular thread that was important at the time. Afterwards, we transcribed the data we collected.

Michael's mother agreed to be interviewed over the phone, once a week, by Sue Lehr. As the mother of an adult son with a disability, Sue is uniquely qualified to talk with parents and develop the rapport needed for this project. As it was impossible to record these calls, Sue kept detailed handwritten notes and recorded her impressions after every session. It soon became clear that Michael's mother looked forward to their conversations. It was the first time she had ever shared such intimate details of her family life with anyone. Eventually she invited Sue to spend a day with her in person at her home. Mrs. Kennedy gathered family photos and mementoes and invited a variety of family members to visit with Sue and complete the story she wanted to tell.

Michael exercised his rights under the Freedom of Information Act to obtain his official records from the New York State agencies involved in his care. While these records were far from complete, we were able to piece together an official timeline of diagnosis and confinement during his early years. We examined intake evaluations, discharge summaries, and Michael's few remaining school records. No documents covering his physical care during his years at Rome Developmental Center came to light. During those years, Michael's physical condition deteriorated markedly and he developed numerous medical problems that likely resulted from a lack of care and general poor health due to living in close quarters with others. Daily logs that might have provided concrete evidence of abuse were no longer extant, and we found no official records of physical injuries caused by the alleged caregivers. We did find several individuals who corroborated Michael's stories of abuse convincingly, however. We also know that the treatment Michael experienced was endemic in institutions from the 1960s and 1970s, as works like *The Willowbrook Wars* and *Christmas in Purgatory* clearly document.

Lori Kennedy, Michael's wife, was eager to share her story of their marriage. An articulate professional, Lori contributed a wealth of detail about their daily life and challenges and helped to verify many of the events Michael recalled. Just as they did with Michael, Sue and Janet usually interviewed Lori for about an hour at a time and then transcribed the recorded data afterward. Although she was initially uncertain about using her real name, in the end Lori came to regard the chance to chronicle major life events as a liberating experience.

Since Michael lived in two different institutions for most of his childhood and early adolescence, we felt it was important to learn as much as possible about both settings. In some respects, institutions are all the same, but Rome Developmental Center's history and reputation diverged from that of Syracuse Developmental Center in a number of significant ways. When Michael moved there, Syracuse Developmental Center was thriving as a center of innovative thinking about the care and welfare of persons with disabilities. Interestingly, Rome State School had once enjoyed a similar reputation as a cutting-edge, progressive place, but it had degenerated into a prison-like institution known for its negative atmosphere and backwardness. Through our interviews with key reformers, professionals who either worked at Syracuse Developmental Center at the time or were involved in changing the system during the deinstitu-tionalization movement, we sought to identify the reasons why SDC accomplished what Rome State School had promised more than fifty years earlier. We also reviewed records kept in the SDC Museum, the Burton Blatt Institute Archives, and the New York State Archives.

Michael has spent the past twenty years as a public figure in the self-advocacy movement. A graduate research assistant took on the task of compiling information from the numerous newspaper stories and documentaries about him in addition to conference proceedings that recorded his speeches. We used this information to comprehend his early work as a new self-advocate and his growing confidence as a professional speaker, trainer, and activist.

Many people played a role in bringing this project to fruition, but Michael was a key player in every step of the process, from brain-storming about the best way to approach the project to the final formatting. His open, honest and self-critical attitude set the tone for the entire endeavor. He was always willing to explain and elaborate on stories he had told and he demonstrated unbelievable patience during the seemingly endless editing process, when Sherry asked for another week, then another month, and finally just one more week to finish editing the text. Although the book required a collaborative effort, it worked only because Michael made it work. There is no doubt that this is Michael's book, his story of his life in institutions and the way he forged his own way out.

Endnotes

[1] Unless otherwise indicated, all of the people in this book are referred to by their real names, with their permission.

[2] Robbie, the Kennedy's fourth child, was born when Michael was one year old.

[3] For more on Little's work, see Barry S. Schifrin and Lawrence D. Longo, "William John Little and cerebral palsy: A reappraisal", *European Journal of Obstetrics & Gynecology and Reproductive Biology* 90 (2000) 139–144.

[4] Christos Panteliadis, Panos Panteliadis and Frank Vassilyadi, "Hallmarks in the history of cerebral palsy: From antiquity to mid-20th century", *Brain & Development* 35 (2013) 289–290.

[5] It was not until the early 1980s that extensive medical research concluded that, despite some birth trauma among the 35,000 children studied, no consistent cause for cerebral palsy could be identified.

[6] later renamed the Ithaca Special Children's Center

[7] Dr. Newton Schaffer founded the hospital during a tuberculosis epidemic in 1900 that left many children disabled. Today, it is the Helen Hayes Hospital, a nationally known rehabilitation center. See helenhayeshospital.org/aboutHHH/history_mission.htm for more information.

[8] Perhaps the most damning assessment came from Bruno Bettelheim, noted psychoanalyst and author of *The Empty Fortress* (New York: Free Press, 1967), who blamed mothers for creating children with autism by being emotionally distant, cold, aloof and uncaring. Although subsequent research has revealed how misguided

and judgmental this accusation was, at the time it was viewed as scientifically valid.

[9] Pearl S. Buck, *The Child Who Never Grew*. 2nd. edition. Training School at Vineland, New Jersey: Woodbine Press. pp. 43-44.

[10] "The Child Who Never Grew" was also published as a booklet by J. Day Co. in 1950 and later excerpted in both *Reader's Digest* and *Time Magazine* (Trent, p. 231). See also Shawn E. Christ and Stanley Finger, "Pearl S. Buck and Phenylketonuria," *The World of PKU: A PKU Knowledgebase*, http://www.pkuworld.org/.

[11] Interestingly, nearly all of these articles were directed at mothers; fathers seemed to have no familial role as such.

[12] Dale Evans Rogers, *Angel Unaware: A Touching Story of Love and Loss*, (Grand Rapids, MI: Revell, 1953). Evans donated the royalties from the sale of this book to the fledgling organization known then as the National Association for Retarded Children.

[13] Letter from Charles Wilbur to W.H.C. Smith, May 1909, quoted in Trent, 97.

[14] The facility was originally a poorhouse, built in 1827. Sarah Frances Rose, *No Right to be Idle: The Invention of Disability, 1850--1930*, Dissertation (Ann Arbor: ProQuest, 2008) 100-101.

[15] Charles Bernstein, "Discussion of [Mason paper]," *Proceedings of New York State Conference of Charities and Corrections* 4 (1903): 201.

[16] Rose, 113.

[17] Philip Ferguson, *Abandoned to Their Fate: Social Policy and Practice Toward Severely Retarded People in America, 1820-1920*. (Philadelphia: Temple UP, 1994), 114-17.

[18] Rome Asylum, *Ninth Annual Report*, 1903, 25.

[19] A pseudonym

[20] TA Living Unit, Case Review, April 12, 1978

[21] OTR, Case Review, April 12, 1978

[22] Speech & Hearing Assistant II, Case Review, October 5, 1977.

[23] Senior Recreation Therapist, Case Review, October 5, 1977

[24] Senior Speech and Hearing Therapist, Case Review, April 12, 1978

[25] Social Worker, Case review, October 5, 1977

[26] Teacher, Case Review, October 5, 1977

[27] Social Worker, Case review, October 5, 1977

[28] For an overview of the provisions of this landmark law and subsequent legal changes, see Office of Special Education Programs, *History: Twenty-Five Years of Progress in Educating Children with Disabilities through IDEA.* (Washington: US Department of Education, 2000) http://www2.ed.gov/policy/speced/leg/idea/history.pdf

[29] Social Worker, Case Review, April 12, 1978

[30] A pseudonym

[31] Teacher, Case Review, October 5, 1977

[32] TA Living Unit, Case Review, April 12, 1978

[33] In 1955, Willowbrook housed 3600 residents, though its official capacity was 2950; by 1963, the institution had been expanded to accommodate 4275 people but 6000 actually lived there.

[34] Helen Starogiannis and Darryl B. Hill. "Sex and Gender in an American State School (1951–1987): The Willowbrook Class." *Sexuality & Disability* 26, no. 2 (June 2008): 83-103.

[35] "Excerpts from statements by Kennedy." *New York Times*, Sept. 10, 1965, p. 21.

[36] For example, "State sued in death of retarded boy, 6", *New York Times*, December 1, 1965, p. 41; L. Van Gelder, "Two attendants at Willowbrook accused of beating 3 patients", *New York Times* December 7, 1972, p. 44; and "Mentally retarded patient, 12, raped", *New York Times* April 29, 1973, p. 34.

[37] For graphic descriptions of conditions in other institutions, see Burton Blatt and Fred Kaplan, *Christmas in Purgatory: A Photographic essay on mental retardation* (Boston: Allyn & Bacon, 1966); reprinted by Human Policy Press, 1974.

[38] A copy of the consent decree may be viewed at http://www.library.csi.cuny.edu/archives/pdfs/consent%20decree.pdf

[39] Willowbrook Consent Decree, p. 3 (http://www.library.csi.cuny.edu/archives/pdfs/consent%20decree.pdf)

[40] Education for All Handicapped Children Act of 1975, §20 USC 1401 §3b,c. The text of the Act is available at http://www.gpo.gov/fdsys/pkg/STATUTE-89/pdf/STATUTE-89-Pg773.pdf41 Education for All Handicapped Children Act of 1975, §20 USC 1401 §4 (16).

[42] See Chapter 7.

[43] In fact, RDC was already downsizing in preparation for closing its doors permanently; like Willowbrook, RDC stood little chance of fulfilling the requirements set forth in the Consent Decree.

[44] The Syracuse Branch of the United Cerebral Palsy Association later changed its name to ENABLE.

[45] Part of the following narrative has been excerpted from an unpublished article Michael wrote with Zana Marie Lutfiyya and Rachael Zubal in the early 1990s.

[46] Pat Killius and Michael Kennedy, "Who we are – personal views", *The Self-Advocacy Advisor* (February 1995) p. 2.

[47] Ibid, 2.

[48] Ibid, 2.

[49] TASH stands for The Association for the Severely Handicapped. Like the NAACP, the organization has retained the acronym even though the terms it signifies are obsolete.

[50] Lou Brown, "Who are they and what do they want? An essay on TASH"; Wayne Sailor, "History", *TASH: Equal Opportunity and Inclusion for People with Disabilities.* http://tash.org/about/history/ accessed 11/1/2013.

[51] Ibid.

[52] Sailor, http://tash.org/about/history/.

[53] "Self Advocacy Advisor" February 1995. Reprinted at http://www.tbiwa.org/wp-content/uploads/2013/02/ADVISOR-2.pdf, accessed 1 November 2013.

[54] Case summary, *Homeward Bound v. Hissom Memorial Center* (85-C-437 N.D. Oklahoma). University of Michigan Law School: The Civil Rights Litigation Clearinghouse. http://www.clearinghouse.net/detail.php?id=487.

[55] Michael's other former roommate, Oscar, remained in Syracuse, but eventually became disabled himself. He and Michael drifted apart over the years, and Michael has not heard from him since Paul's death.

[56] Steve Luxenberg, Annie's ghosts: A journey into a family secret. New York: Hyperion, 2009 1.

References

Atkinson, D. (December 2004). Research and empowerment: involving people with learning difficulties in oral and life history research. *Disability and Society*. 19:7, 691-702.

Beart, S., Hardy, G., & Burchan, L. (2004). Changing selves: A grounded theory account of belonging to a self-advocacy group for people with intellectual disabilities. *Journal of Applied Research in Intellectual Disabilities*. 17: 91-100.

Beam, Alex. (2001). *Gracefully Insane - Life and death inside America's Premier Mental Hospital*. New York: Public Affairs.

Bernstein, Charles. (1903) "Discussion of [Mason paper]," *Proceedings of New York State Conference of Charities and Corrections* 4: 201.

Bettelheim, Bruno (1967). *The empty fortress: Infantile autism and the birth of the self*. New York, NY: The Free Press.

Blatt, Burton & Kaplan, Fred. (1974). *Christmas in Purgatory - A photographic essay on mental retardation*. Syracuse, NY: Human Policy Press.

Brown, Lou. Who are they and what do they want? An essay on TASH-Equity, Opportunity and inclusion for People with Disabilities. www.tash.org.

Buck, Pearl S., (1992). *The Child Who Never Grew*. 2nd. edition. Vineland, New Jersey: Woodbine Press.

Case summary, *Homeward Bound v. Hissom Memorial Center* (85-C-437 N.D. Oklahoma). University of Michigan Law School: The Civil Rights Litigation Clearinghouse, http://www.clearinghouse.net/detail.php?id=487.

Christ, Shawn E. and Stanley Finger, "Pearl S. Buck and Phenylketonuria," *The World of PKU: A PKU Knowledgebase*, http://www.pkuworld.org/.

D'Antonio, Michael. (2004). *The state boys rebellion - the inspiring story of American eugenics and the men who overcame it*. New York: Simon & Shuster Paperbacks.

Dostoevsky, Fyodor. (2003). *The idiot. The new translation by Richard Pevear and Larissa Volokhonsky*. New York: Vintage Books.

Dowse, L. (2001). Contesting practices, challenging codes: self-advocacy, disability politics and the social model. *Disability & Society*. 16:1, 123-141.

Evans Rogers, Dale. (1953) *Angel Unaware: A Touching Story of Love and Loss*. Grand Rapids, MI: Revell.

Ferguson. L., & Ferguson, P.M. (2011). "The promise of adulthood" in M.E. Snell & F. Brown (Eds.). *Instruction of students with severe disabilities* (7th ed.) Columbus, OH: Person/Merrill Prentice-Hall.

Ferguson, Philip. (1994) *Abandoned to their Fate: Social policy and practice toward severely retarded people in America, 1820-1920*. Philadelphia: Temple UP.

Galvin, R. (August, 2003). The paradox of disability culture: the need to combine versus the imperative to let go. *Disability & Society*. 18(5), 675-690.

Geller, J.L., & Harris, M. (1994). *Women of the asylum - Voices from behind the walls - 1840-1945*. New York: Anchor Book/Doubleday.

Kennedy, Michael J. (24 March 1992) Promotes Awareness: 'Nancy' aids cause of the disabled. *Syracuse Herald Journal*.

Kennedy, Michael J. (25 September 1999) Wants to marry without government interference. *Accent on Living*. 38 (2). 20-22.

Killius, Patricia and Michael J. Kennedy. (February 1995) "Who we are – personal views". *The Self-Advocacy Advisor*. Reprinted at http://www.tbiwa.org/wp-content/uploads/2013/02/ADVISOR-2.pdf.

Leece, J. (September 2007). Direct payments and user-controlled support: The challenges for social care commissioning. *Practice*. 19:3, 185-199.

Lewis, Mindy (2002). *Life inside - A memoir*. New York: Washington Square Press.

Little, D., (Winter 2010). Identity, efficacy, and disability rights movement recruitment. *Disability Studies Quarterly*. 30:1, 2-21.

Luxenberg, Steve (2009). *Annie's ghosts: A journey into a family secret*. New York: Hyperion.

Mills, B., (Winter 2010). "Nothing about us, without us." Book Review. *Disability Studies Quarterly*. 30(1), 7-7.

Moore, S. A., Melchior, L., & Davis, J.M. (2008). 'Me and the 5 P's': negotiating rights-based critical disabilities studies and social inclusion. *International Journal of Children's Rights*. 16: 249-262.

Office of Special Education Programs. (2000) *History: Twenty-Five Years of Progress in Educating Children with Disabilities through IDEA*. Washington, DC: US Department of Education. http://www2. ed.gov/policy/speced/leg/idea/history.pdf

Owens, J. (May 2007). Liberating voices through narrative methods: the case for an interpretive research approach. *Disability and Society*. 22:3, 299-313.

Panteliadis, Christos, Panos Panteliadis and Frank Vassilyadi. (2013). Hallmarks in the history of cerebral palsy: From antiquity to mid-20th century. *Brain & Development* 35: 285-292.

Parish, S.L., & Lutwick, Z. (October 2005). A critical analysis of the emerging crisis in long-term care for people with developmental disabilities. *Social Work*. 50:4, 345-354.

Patterson, Orlando. (1991). *Freedom in the making of western culture*. New York: Basic Books.

Rose, Sarah Frances. (2008) *No Right to be Idle: The Invention of Disability, 1850—1930*. Dissertation. Ann Arbor: ProQuest.

Rose-Ackerman, S. (October 1982). Mental retardation and society: The ethics and politics of normalization. *Ethics*. 93:1, 88-101.

Rothman, D. J. & Rothman, S. M. (1984). *The Willowbrook wars: Bringing the mentally disabled into the community*. New York, NY: Harper Row.

Sailor, Wayne. Commentary on Self-advocacy. www.tash.org.

Schifrin, Barry S. and Lawrence D. Longo. (2000). William John Little and cerebral palsy: A reappraisal. *European Journal of Obstetrics & Gynecology and Reproductive Biology* 90: 139–144.

Schiller, Lori, & Bennett, Amanda (1996). *A journey out of the torment of madness.* New York: Warner Books.

Schoultz, Bonnie. (undated). *More thoughts on self-advocacy: The Movement, the group, and the Individual.* National Resource Center on Community Integration, Center on Human Policy, School of Education, Syracuse University, through the U.S. Department of Education, Office of Special Education and Rehabilitation Services. National Institute on Disability and Rehabilitation.

Sherry, M. (September 2004). Review of The disability rights movement: From deinstitutionalization to self-determination by Duane F. Stroman. *Contemporary Sociology.* 33:5, 589-590.

Smith, P., & Routel, C. (Winter 2010). Transition failure: the cultural bias of self-determination and the journey to adulthood for people with disabilities. *Disabilities Studies Quarterly.* 30:1, 1-11.

Starogiannis, Helen and Darryl B. Hill. (June 2008) Sex and Gender in an American State School (1951–1987): The Willowbrook Class. *Sexuality & Disability* 26:2, 83-103.

Thompson, D. (2002). "Well, we've all got to get old haven't we?" Reflections of older people with intellectual disabilities on aging and change. *Journal of Gerontological Social Work.* 37:3/4, 7-23.

Trent, James W., Jr. (1994). *Inventing the feeble mind - A history of mental retardation in the United States.* Berkeley, CA: University of California Press.

Tuller, J. (no date). Olmstead and self-determination. National Self-Determination Program Office. www.self-determination.org.

Walker, P. M., & Rogan, P. (2007). *Make the day matter! Promoting typical lifestyles for adults with significant disabilities.* Baltimore, MD: Paul H. Brookes Publishing Company.

"What do members want from People First?" (undated). Research Center on Community Living. Center on Human Policy. Syracuse University. Syracuse, NY.

"What is self-advocacy?" (undated). National Resource Center on Supported Living and Choice. Center on Human Policy. Syracuse University, Syracuse, NY

CPSIA information can be obtained at www.ICGtesting.com
Printed in the USA
BVOW03s0201080714

358453BV00002B/12/P